C000265431

STEVE INCE

COLLECTED
GAME WRITING
ARTICLES

Dedication

To Laura MacDonald,
a truly supportive friend.

Contents

Introduction

A career spanning 30 years is not insubstantial, particularly when you consider that I didn't enter the games industry until I was 35. In many ways I was very fortunate to be given a chance to prove myself and build from there.

Because of the experience and knowledge I began to amass, I thought it only right that I share it with others in the hope that those readers might benefit to some degree.

I've never been a fan of the type of article that takes a stance of "this is how it must be done" as there is rarely just one way to do things. I try to avoid that approach to my articles but hope they have within them ideas and procedures that resonate to at least part of the audience.

I don't want to tell people how to do things but hopefully demonstrate the kind of things that have worked for me. Perhaps some of them will work for you, too.

I decided to collect these articles in this volume to go with my other game writing books and give a sense of completeness to everything I've written related to games.

The articles were originally published in a variety of places and I've noted each particular place under the title of each one.

I've also included a regular column, Developing Thoughts, that was originally published on Randomville. Although each part is relatively small in itself, they build to a substantial body when collected together.

Every article included (and I hope I haven't missed any) is presented exactly as it was originally written without any editing.

Take care,
Steve Ince, June 2023.

PS – The book's front cover image is a painting I created as a test that contributed to me getting my initial job with Revolution. It's based on a sketch Dave Gibbons drew for the game, *Beneath a Steel Sky*. Alas, my version wasn't the one used in the game.

Part 1
Collected
Articles

My Fingers are Blistered and Bleeding – Writing for games

(Originally published on GIGnews.com)

I once read that Ernest Hemingway, when working on For Whom the Bell Tolls, rewrote the final page thirty-nine times. Such was his desire to capture exactly the right finish to an important piece of work – to give the reader the very best possible experience when reading his book.

Very few of us have the luxury to be such a perfectionist. We do not have Hemingway's unique gift, his well-established reputation, or his complete artistic freedom, and the pressures of time constantly bear down upon us. Yet the professional writer must accept that they are to deliver the very best possible writing at all times – it is only natural that the client expects no less.

Writing is not easy, even for the Ernest Hemingways among us. Good writing – that teasingly wicked and lofty ideal – can be increasingly elusive the more a writer searches the infinite variety of word combinations to find the one that will convey his intention perfectly. When the pressure of looming development deadlines is added to this, it becomes clear that writing well for games is a monumental undertaking, particularly when the sheer scale of a typical game project is factored in.

That's a lot of words.

The word count requirement for a game can be huge. Adventures and role-playing games regularly have a line count that is in the high thousands or even tens of thousands, and a word count that can be as high as one hundred thousand or more. It is the writer's task to create those words and deliver a script that's dynamic and exciting, but which also matches the style and vision of the project.

For Broken Sword – The Sleeping Dragon, there were 6,600 lines of dialogue – a running time of between eight and nine hours' worth of samples. Now, if it is assumed that fifty percent of a two-hour movie is dialogue (this will vary greatly depending on the movie genre), then for this one game we have the equivalent of eight movie-scripts, written in less than a year. For anyone who's ever tried to write a movie script, this is a pretty sobering, and scary, thought.

From another perspective, there were 60,000 words spoken in the game – the equivalent of a small novel, but without a single word of descriptive prose. Just imagine how big that novel would be if it incorporated each and every spoken word from the game as well as the necessary descriptive passages.

Why on earth would anyone want to write for games?

The answer lies in the nature of creativity itself. It's something that we all have within us to a greater or lesser degree, but which takes on a whole new dimension at the level required when writing for top-quality games.

To be truly creative, a person is driven by the need to create. If not actually directly involved in the creative process at any one moment, then that compulsion will take over their thoughts, distract them in the middle of conversations, and pop ideas into their head while explaining to the bank manager why the loan payment is late. Creativity is their life! They do not have a choice in the matter.

To fulfil the creative urge to its maximum, a person will look for ways to push at the boundaries of their creativity. Games, because of their increasingly changing nature, today offer one of the best chances for a creative individual to explore their own boundaries. For a writer it's an ideal opportunity to innovate in a medium that devours groundbreaking ideas like no other.

Why would any writer want to avoid writing for games when they offer so many real opportunities to feed the hungry urge of their creativity?

What exactly does a game writer do?

It is a strong misconception that the role of the writer is simply that of writing exciting or humorous dialogue. It's perfectly valid that a developer only requires a writer to fulfil that aspect of the project, but there could be others where the skills of a writer would benefit the quality of the project.

While dialogue is incredibly important to get right, it is only part of the overall service that a writer can provide. If the story is weak or the characters poorly defined, then even the best dialogue in the world will always struggle to compensate for this.

Of course, not every game has a need for a rich and complex plot or a villain that has a human, angst-ridden side to contrast with his evil nature. But whatever the level of writing required for a project, the earlier a writer can be brought in and contribute to maintaining a consistent vision, the better the final product will be.

Brainstorming sessions are a valuable way of both letting the writer contribute in a broader sense and allowing the writer to start working with the design team in a constructive manner from the outset. It also has the benefit of allowing the team to get to know the writer and what he's like to work with in general.

There is always an awful lot of documentation that has to be undertaken during the course of the project's development, particularly in the early stages. The design team will write much of the documentation, but a writer can provide a valuable service by offering an objective eye on the documents created. A writer could even be employed to edit or re-write them if there is concern that a lack of clarity may lead to misunderstandings between the various departments in the company. Such problems would be disastrous if they led to re-work and wasted time.

Many, if not all, games are signed up based on a successful proposal document. A writer, particularly one who understands the development process, can be particularly valuable here by helping the developer to write a document that is clear and to the point, delivering the relevant information in a dynamic exciting manner.

The value of professional writers

Clearly, writing for games is an incredibly demanding task, and certainly not one to be undertaken lightly. If we are to create games that get even halfway to Hemingway's standard, writing, and the writers themselves, must be seen as a valuable commodity.

There is a reluctance to embrace this fully, with frequent opinion that to employ the services of a writer is an expensive luxury. Happily, there is evidence of changing attitudes towards this and more developers are using specialist writers to match the high standards expected in all other aspects of game development. Those developers who do not recognise the value of a professional writer will be at a disadvantage if they hope to compete in an increasingly demanding marketplace.

Having been instrumental in developing the design of a number of quality games, I am a firm believer that the writing undertaken should always be approached from the standpoint of how best to complement the gameplay. Only by achieving this will the writer have succeeded in their task. As a professional, satisfactory completion of that task means delivering on a promise made to the client. Just as the best film writers understand the process of making a film, so the best game writers must understand the processes involved in developing a game. Only then will they truly maximise their creativity and prove their true worth to the developer.

Accepting the value of a writer is only part of the issue. Like every other important task in the development project, the correct amount of time has to be allowed for in the schedule if the writer is to maximise the quality of the work he delivers.

Good writing not only requires the skills of the writer, but also the time in which to create it.

So how does a person get to write for games?

Unfortunately, it's becoming increasingly difficult to write for games without some kind of track record. Greater demands for professional, proven writers means that a developer is going to look first at writers of other quality games or writers from film and television that they believe can work with them in the manner required.

All is not bleak, however, though you may need to be prepared for a hard slog or have to prove yourself from within the industry before being given your chance. The Game Writers' Special Interest Group of IGDA offers some very good advice (http://www.igda.org/writing/HowDoYouBecomeAGa meWriter.htm) which basically boils down to four choices – join a script agency; become part of a larger team of writers in an apprenticeship role; work from within a developer; write for other media first.

Of course, getting a book, television or film credit is a difficult proposition in itself, but such are the high standards required of game professionals in all areas, that to say otherwise would ignore the rapidly changing nature of game development.

A more appealing alternative may be to write your own game and publish it yourself. It then becomes your calling card and proof that you can write, particularly if you are able to get strong reviews. Now this may seem a daunting task, but Jonathan Boakes created Dark Fall on his own and received great acclaim for it.

Unlike the film industry, where anyone can write a script and submit it to the film studios, there is no real equivalent in the game industry – they are simply not set up, in the main, for that kind of approach. A writer does not produce the "screenplay" for a game and then a studio makes the game. A development studio creates a proposal for a game, then brings a writer on board as the project requires it, sometimes at the point of developing the proposal itself.

Having said all that, my own path to becoming a writer in the game industry was a somewhat circuitous one. Arriving relatively late in life at the age of 34, I actually entered the industry as an artist, such was the direction my creative compulsion took me at that time. With some published short stories and poetry behind me, I'd always had an interest in and a love of writing, but it was from within the industry itself that I saw the fabulous opportunities that lay before me. My creative drive increasingly shifted from art to writing and opened up within me a depth I'd been unaware of until that point.

Working alongside other talented writers, from the start of my time in the industry, was a great source of inspiration and contributed enormously to my own development. Certainly, without the encouragement and the catalysing effect they had on my development as a writer, I wouldn't be in the position I am today.

So where does that leave you, the aspiring game writer? Like writing in any field, you have to be prepared for the long haul, with clear goals and a plan that should adapt with the changing face of the industry. The key to your success will be a firm belief in your talent as a writer and the conviction that writing for a highly interactive medium is what you yearn to do.

Interaction Density – Has the Player Got Plenty To Do?

(First published on biz.gamedaily.com)

For a long time now, people have been writing off the adventure game genre as dead or dying. It's increasingly frustrating that people would feel this way – particularly about a genre that was once one of the most popular – until you realise that many game players feel adventure games are boring. But why would players think so when so much care and attention goes into the creation of these games?

I recently read Lisa Sikora's My Turn article, *Content is Queen* and my initial thought was that adventures should be pulling in the female gamer like no other genre. If it was simply down to content, this would indeed be the case. For instance, a number of adventure games contain far deeper, richer female characters than Alyx from Half Life 2. Kate from Syberia and April from The Longest Journey are two examples that immediately spring to mind.

So, if we already have the richness of content, with stories that are regularly more complex and involving than any found in even the best action game, and empathic female characters, why is it that adventures are failing to appeal to the female gamer in large numbers? What is it about them that fails to appeal to gamers in general?

A large part of the answer is, I believe, a lack of Interaction Density. By this, I mean that there simply isn't enough for the player to do at any one time.

If you make your own soft drinks by adding fruit concentrate to water, or to carbonated water in one of those fizzy-drink-making machines, and don't follow the directions or use quality concentrate, the drink you make always disappoints. Buying cheap varieties of concentrate or eking out the expensive concentrate never gives you the flavour that you desire. The problem with eking out even the best concentrate is that the more you do so, the worse the flavour tastes, until you reach a point where plain old tap water actually tastes better than the over-diluted drink.

In the drink we call video games, Interaction Density is the fruit concentrate that gives the rich flavour we all crave. If Interaction Density is not high enough, the gameplay feels diluted and doesn't satisfy our needs for a game filled with a rich flavour of regular input.

I'm sure we've all seen comments in forums and articles which suggest that games aren't as much fun as they used to be. This is often interpreted as a nostalgia-influenced feeling, or that recent games genuinely lack the quality of gameplay their predecessors had. I believe that, although there may be an element of these things, in the main it's unlikely to be the case.

To me, the quality of the gameplay is high in the vast majority of games, but often that quality is being spread too thinly.

If we look back to the early 1990s, much of the size of a game was limited by the fact that they were published on floppy discs. This meant that every location or level in a game was made to work hard for its keep. For an adventure game, each of the labs, bars, shops, alleys, etc was filled with items to collect, characters to talk with and background objects to examine. Gaining access to a new location was always such fun in itself because the player would spend time simply interacting with the environment and everything within it. When this exploratory interaction was combined with the actual gameplay of working through the developing story, it meant there was always plenty the player could find to do at any given moment. Even when the player became stuck on a puzzle, they generally knew that the solution would be fairly close by because there were only a handful of locations you were likely able to visit.

As technology has progressed and the delivery of games now happens through the media of CDs or DVDs, the amount of game world that the player can explore has increased tremendously. On the face of it, the idea of having a large world to investigate has an immediate appeal, but the downside is that, because the amount of gameplay has not increased in proportion, the Interaction Density has reduced to a point where plain old tap water is looking pretty good.

Wandering around large, open environments quickly pales if there is nothing of interest to occupy the player's attention. How long will the player wander through snowy mountains or along desert paths before the lack of interaction opportunities makes even the best location graphics seem dull?

There are plenty of games which suggest their creators understand the problem of low Interaction Density, even if it's only on an intuitive level. However, the common solution often appears to be one of filling the game with generic, repetitive gameplay. The best games, of course, use this generic gameplay well and vary the setups and scenarios to create the variety the player craves from the generic components. Half-Life 2 is probably the current best example of this. Where I think games abuse their own generic gameplay is when the player simply has to contend with gameplay that's either been thrown together with little thought, or fight through countless random battles that can, at times, become more irritating than having nothing to do.

What, though, happens in an action game when the player has cleared the level of opponents? If they haven't obtained the one item that allows them to progress they could be stuck in a section of the world that now offers them little to interact with. The Interaction Density has suddenly dropped from very high to very low. Providing the player isn't held up for very long, this change of pace can be very welcoming, giving the player the chance for a breather, but could become frustrating if they begin to feel that all they are doing is simply wandering around aimlessly.

In the eyes of many players – particularly those who have come to expect, unknowingly, a high level of Interaction Density – adventure games are increasingly less appealing. Although the creators of all types of games should ensure that the Interaction Density is as high as possible, the creators of adventures have much more work to do to ensure that players have a large number of things to keep them constantly occupied. Adventures, by their traditional definition, cannot rely on the inclusion of generic action gameplay and so must either provide more gameplay within the expanded worlds or compact those worlds to increase the Interaction Density. Adventures do not have bad gameplay, it is simply spread about too sparsely, which has a negative affect on how it is perceived.

A game that provides a rich mixture of content, through a combination of strong story, compelling characters and well-balanced, intelligent gameplay should always draw people in. When all these aspects are delivered in a way that ensures there is always something to keep the player's interest alive, then the creator will have something in which the flavour of the concentrate has not been over-diluted.

Interaction Density cannot create a good game in itself, if the points of interest, the things the player can do, are not of sufficient quality. But if the quality of gameplay is great, the full flavour of high Interaction Density may just be something for which the player develops a real taste.

A Day in the Life – Monday 7th March 2005

(Originally published on Gamasutra.com)

Because I work from home, I thought that I would put that work into a larger context and cover the whole of my day from waking till going to bed again. There are times in the day when it can be difficult to demarcate the boundary between what is my time and what is the client's because I regularly think about the current work while doing mundane chores around the house.

There is no specific reason that I chose the day I did, but it's pretty typical of how I spend my time. When I work on something like story or character development, I work very intensely and breaks will fit themselves around the work itself, which is why so many of the times are odd ones.

It's very important to be self-disciplined when working from home. For me this means proper planning with the client to come up with a series of deadlines that we are both happy with. In order that I reach those deadlines without undue pressure, I always make sure that I have a structured day to maximise the amount of time spent on the client's work.

7am

The alarm clock goes off at the same time every day. It's a battered old thing that must be at least fifteen years old, but it does its job and wakes me up every morning.

I regularly wake before the alarm sounds and will lie in bed thinking about the day ahead, particularly if the previous day's writing hit a tricky patch. This peaceful time is often when the best solutions to these problems come to me.

Although I'm a morning person and like to get up early, the reason the alarm is set is for my partner, June, who works in the council offices about 20 miles away and needs to be there by 8:30. As I'm always quickest to rouse, I make us a cup of tea. It's been particularly cold recently so I light the gas fire in the living room. Breakfast consists of a bowl of cereal. June and I spend about twenty minutes together before she prepares herself for work.

7.25

While June takes the first turn in the bathroom, I boot up my computer and check my e-mails and update my site if I have anything prepared from the previous evening. I've just started up a new comic strip in a simple style which allows me to put the individual strips together very quickly. I like to have a presence on the web that has a connection to my career, but at the same time is separate. At some point during this period, June will enter my office and bid me a fond farewell for the day.

8.02

My turn in the bathroom and although taking a shower doesn't last long, it's another chance to do some thinking and I come up with a neat development I can work into the story I am currently developing. The shower is followed by a shave, after which I realise that the wheelie bin needs putting out front – the council informed us only last week that the day of refuse collection was being changed from Friday to Monday, so although the bin was only emptied a few days earlier, I found something to put into it so that they would still have something to do.

I always put food out for the wild birds as I like to watch them feeding. We get quite a variety – three types of tit, two types of finch, robins, sparrows, thrushes and blackbirds. I saw a woodpecker for the first time the other day, but it hasn't been back since.

8.35

Before I launch into my work, I like to browse a few gaming websites. When you work from home it's vitally important that you keep up on all the latest gaming news as it happens. I find that trying to catch up once a week can be a little overwhelming. Sometime it seems as though the whole landscape of gaming changes three times from Monday to Friday.

9.05

Start work. The first ten or fifteen minutes is spent reading over the work I completed on Friday, during which I spot a couple of phrases that need a little re-wording for clarity. Overall, though, I'm pleased with the flow and get back into the rhythm very quickly.

My current client is an excellent company who brought me in to work on the story and story-related content for an action game. The key with this type of story development is to do so in a way that enriches the experience and complements the action.

I'm currently working on the second draft of the main story, which has turned out to be surprisingly rich, and I'm working through the client's feedback on the first draft, as well as incorporating new gameplay details they have developed since the first draft was started. Feedback and answers to questions are very swift at coming through, which is important if a writer is to deliver what the client wants.

Like the first person shooter I did story work for at the end of last year, this client had the structure of the story mapped out but felt that they needed to bring someone else in to help enrich it and develop the characters to a greater degree. When this is the case, the story work takes place over a much shorter period than if the story had been created from scratch.

Though the story document is not for wider publication, I like to write it as dramatically as possible. The intention with this is that all the other members of the team can see how the dynamic nature of the story will complement the exciting gameplay.

I'm quickly adding in some new stuff based upon the gameplay detail and it's coming together very well. The words just seem to flow from my fingers and by the time an hour is up I've written a thousand words.

Though the current work is story revision, the work will vary depending on the client's requirements. Last week it was first draft story work. Next week I'll be working on character profiles. Another client may want a script editing and polishing.

10.12

An e-mail arrives that has a vague offer of a potential job in Denmark. But when I read further I realise that they are looking for level designers. This is quite a regular occurrence – because I call myself a writer-designer, many people seem to think that level design work is part of that. Though there can be an overlap, much level design involves working with 3D software, which is not my speciality.

I spend the next fifteen minutes reviewing the work I've just done.

10.31

I take a short break to make myself a cup of tea and to have a piece of fruit. It's probably because I have breakfast so early, but I find that if I don't eat something at this point of the day I can become a little distracted. In the kitchen I am greeted by a howling cat who clearly has the same idea as I do – she wants something to eat.

While the kettle is boiling I eat a banana and watch the birds feeding through the patio doors. For a brief moment I wonder about the possibility of developing a bird-feeding game, but cannot think, for the moment, how that might work.

10.44

I return to work with my cup of tea sitting on the desk in front of me. I've been known to get wrapped up in the work to the point where the tea goes cold, but today I drink it quite quickly as I think about the next section and how best to put across the new ideas.

Sometimes writing is more about thinking things through than actually doing the typing. Because I type reasonably quickly, producing the work is rarely about getting the words down in time, but in deciding what ideas, feelings and relationships the words will convey.

11.09

The time the post arrives varies quite a bit from day to day, but is usually somewhere between 11am and noon. So when the letter-box rattles I go to check it out in case someone has sent me lots of money, but there's only a letter from the council explaining its new recycling policies – I will read it in detail later.

I return to work and after a short while the new approach to the section I'm working on begins to click and it's not long before the writing is flowing again.

11.24

I'm interrupted by a knock on the door, which breaks my flow. Though I'm tempted not to answer it, you never know when it could be something important. It was only a guy asking if I needed any pruning work done in the garden. As I tend to do these jobs myself I had to turn him away.

One of the disadvantages of working from home is that you get distractions like these all the time, so you need to develop the discipline to be able to get back into the swing of things as quickly as possible.

12.02

I manage to pick up straight away and get a good half hour in before I reach a convenient point at which to break for lunch. It's a little earlier than I'd like, but I like to fit to the flow of the work as much as I'm able.

Lunch consists of some lean ham with a tomato and cucumber salad. I try to eat fairly healthily as much as possible. I'm not fanatical about it, but definitely feel better if I have a varied diet with plenty of fruit and vegetables. As I let the food settle for ten minutes I'll either read the paper or catch up on the news on TV.

12.28

I take half an hour in each day to go for a brisk walk. Because I sit at the computer all day, it's very easy to get into the habit of not taking any exercise, and as I'm a little overweight anyway I'd soon balloon up.

I pick up a couple of pints of milk and some fresh meat for the evening meal. I regularly try to coincide the walk with a visit to the shops; it's an extra encouragement to go out, particularly in winter when the rain and snow may be a little off-putting.

When I return I notice that the daffodils are nearly out, which hopefully means that spring is on the way.

13.05

Back to work on more story refinement. Much of this section of work consists of fleshing out the existing material and refining it, which goes very well.

14.13

I receive an e-mail from another client about a couple of days work I'm to do next week on a fun children's title. One of the advantages of a small job like this one is that I'm able to fit it into the down time on the main job where I'm waiting for feedback. It's always very useful to be on the lookout for this kind of work. It only takes me a minute to reply and then I'm back on the job in hand.

14.44

I take ten minutes out to make myself another cup of tea. The last half hour has moved along very well and I'm surprised at where the time has gone. I notice that a squirrel is perched on the bird table and eating the peanuts. It is completely unfazed as I stare at it through the window.

14.58

Returning to work once more, progress initially goes well then hits a tough patch where I'm forced to unravel ideas from the previous version and weave in the new ideas. I need to tread carefully in case I introduce inconsistencies or plot flaws.

15.46

I receive an e-mail from an adventure game developer who, among other things, asks how well Wanted: a Wild Western Adventure is doing. This was a game that I script edited last year and for which I do not have any figures, so I cannot help his curiosity out.

15.50

I spend the next fifteen minutes checking back and forth between documents and am soon pretty sure that I'm able to continue with the changes in a manner that will work well.

16.05

The client sends me some updated character art for reference, based on changes to one of the main characters we'd talked about previously. It's real quality work and perfectly fits the image I have in my head for the character. Pleased that the visual ideas are complementing the story ideas, I return to the writing with renewed vigour.

I cut out whole sections of the old stuff and work in the new ideas. The careful thoughts from a little while earlier is paying off and once again my fingers rattle across the keyboard as the words flow like a river. After about an hour I've finished all the changes and then review what I've just done.

17.25

I come to a convenient finishing point. Tomorrow I will review the whole document and polish it before passing it onto the client.

17.30

I answer some e-mails that have been building during the day and which didn't need my attention at the time.

17.50

I start the preparation of the evening meal, timing it to be complete for when June arrives home from work.

18.25

June and I sit down together to eat and to share what each of us have done during the day. One of the disadvantages of working from home is the lack of contact with other colleagues that you naturally have when employed within company offices. So I almost find I'm living the office politics vicariously through June.

19.10

I wash the dishes. June and I have an arrangement – I cook and wash the dishes and she washes the clothes and does the ironing. Although this means that I'm doing something every day, I still feel that I get the better deal as ironing is one of the most mind-numbing tasks known to man. The rest of the chores we share.

I have a great idea for a low-budget game while I'm doing the dishes, though not a dish-washing game. I need to explore it some more when I have the time.

19.30

I return to the computer for a while with the idea of doing some work on my comic strip.

19.35

I receive an e-mail from someone asking if I'm going to GDC so that they could set up an interview. Too busy with work to go all the way over to the other side of the States, though I'd love to go one year. I'll have to make do with EGN later this year.

19.45

Remember the game idea and write up a few quick notes so that it doesn't disappear forever.

19.55

Do some work on the comic strip, Mr. Smoozles, and write couple of episode scripts.

20.20

I chat for five minutes on MSN with my son, Jason, about my old laptop and a couple of comics we've both been reading.

20.25

I type up some thoughts I had on a couple of my earlier game ideas. I have more ideas than I'll ever get chance to work on, but they are all valuable and even if they aren't used directly they could feed into other projects.

21.00

I watch TV with June. There's a documentary on the TV about a guy who was a serial bigamist, ruining lots of women's lives in the process. This is followed by ER. Although it's a little like a soap opera most of the time, it's still a well put together programme that always conveys such energy and exciting drama, even in the quietest moments.

23.05

Bedtime. It takes me a while to get to sleep, though, as I think about the work I've been doing during the day...

We Live In Interesting Times

(Originally published on adventuregamers.com)

Interesting times can give rise to very mixed fortunes. The current economic recession is a prime example of that, with the games industry as a whole faring better than many others, although numerous companies have laid off staff and still others have closed altogether. There has been a lot of tightening of belts, and I'm sure we all feel for those who have lost out, but generally speaking there is much to be excited about.

Even in the backwater that is the adventure genre we can see exciting and positive things ahead. It's as if some have (re)discovered the map that brings them here, while others have not even realised the map exists and found their way here anyway, blazing a trail from a different direction. Still others are going to find that they're about to crash land here whether they like it or not.

Just in case you're reading this and wondering what the hell I'm wittering on about ("Ince has finally lost it, shocker"), please bear with me and I'll hopefully make myself clear.

There have been a number of recent developments that, on their own, may not seem remarkable news for the adventure genre, but taken together they offer up an interesting potential trend, and hopefully something for all of us to look forward to.

Okay, the first of these developments IS directly related to the genre and caught many by surprise (except a good friend of mine who kind of predicted it last year) – good old LucasArts has realised that there is still a lot of potential wrapped up in their old adventure IPs. With a re-working of the first *Monkey Island* game and a new series of *Monkey Island* games from Telltale Games, suddenly the adventure genre is news again and journalists using the 'D' word when writing about adventures are notably fewer in number. Did we enter the Twilight Zone at some point in the last couple of months?

The LucasArts development follows hard on the heels of an increasing number of adventure games appearing on so-called "casual" gaming portals. Some of them are re-releases of older adventure games and others are hidden object games that have incorporated adventure gameplay elements in them, and many bear more than a passing resemblance to games like *Myst*. If you look at the top ten of Big Fish Games, for example, adventure style gameplay features very heavily in many of the games positioned there, which suggests that players are buying them in healthy numbers. The purists among you may not like this aspect of adventure genre development, but I think it's a path of which we're only at the beginning and it will be interesting to see where it leads over the next couple of years. Perhaps this is something Adventure Gamers can explore in more depth and cover on a more regular basis.

Another recent development (well, recent-ish) is the way Sony have swung their weight behind David Cage's game, *Heavy Rain*. Now, *Fahrenheit* (or *Indigo Prophecy*) was definitely a love it or hate it kind of game with no middle ground, it seems, but you have to take your hat off to Cage for the things he's trying to do. It's better to try and miss the mark than not to try at all. From what we've seen of *Heavy Rain* so far, I'm sure we'd all agree that there's something pretty impressive taking shape here. Yes, there may be questions about the gameplay and whether it even comes close to being an adventure, but it seems to be much more than just a straightforward action game. Fingers crossed. Not that I have a PS3, mind, so it's a bit of a moot point at the moment.

It may seem that I'm covering ground that's already been discussed a number of times before. I've even done so myself with regards to "casual adventures". However, just today (as of writing the first draft of this piece) I saw two items on the internet that, when combined with the above could lead to interesting conclusions if you're prone to seeing things in a similar way.

The first item was the news that family games are now the most popular type in the UK. I know they're mostly talking about games like *Brain Training* and *Wii Fit*, but the fact that in the last year in the UK we've seen TV advertising for the likes of *Professor Layton*, *Hotel Dusk* and *Another Code* shows that Nintendo sees this kind of game as important to developing a broader player base. We've also seen the DS rise as a natural home for the adventure game, but increasingly the Wii also has a lot of potential in this market. There has been the recent release of *Broken Sword* on the Wii (and DS) and later this year will see the release of the Wii/DS version of *So Blonde*. From the outset, dtp realised the potential of this market and wanted a version of the game that wasn't just a straight port but a "re-imagining" of the original story.

Clearly, the markets are broadening for the adventure genre, and that's always going to be a good thing for those of us creating the games, isn't it? Well, maybe. That's where the second of today's items comes in.

On GamesIndustry.biz there is an interview with Ray Muzyka and Greg Zeschuk from BioWare. It's a very interesting read in general, but I was fascinated by the fact that they think we're at the point where AAA game developers can think about dropping combat from their titles and place the games in a more real-world setting. So I started thinking about this a little and what type of games would we be talking about? What kind of games would appeal to a broader demographic?

If you take the combat out of recent *Tomb Raider* games for instance (and if you play them on easy they have very little combat anyway) they just become 3D platform games with a relatively shallow story. This isn't the kind of thing the BioWare guys are referring to because they talk about much richer narrative experiences.

So, let's take a look at one of their own games – *Mass Effect*. Clearly a title deserving of a triple-A billing and one with great scope. If you took out the combat and transposed it to a real-world setting, what would you have? Would it not become an adventure? You could, of course, argue that it would still be an RPG, but without combat and all the skill development that goes along with it, is that really the case?

It seems to me that the only way you can tell a compelling story in a game that's set in the real world and without combat is to make it an adventure. Maybe not quite using controls that we'd be familiar with, but an adventure nonetheless. Personally, I can't wait for it to happen. Oh, wait... it's already happening.

For instance, just take a look at the work that Martin Gantehör and his team are creating over at House of Tales. These are already great looking games – just imagine what those guys could do if they had the kind of budget that BioWare generally have at their disposal.

Better yet, imagine what any of your favourite adventure developers could do with a triple-A budget: Jane Jensen, Telltale Games, Revolution Software, Wizarbox, Autumn Moon, etc. I don't know about you, but I'm smiling just thinking about it.

But – and it's a pretty big but – is this ever likely to happen? When the publishers realise that there's an awful lot of life in our wonderful genre, will they beat paths to our various doors? Or will they give the money to the BioWares of the world who have great experience at producing AAA games but have yet to produce a non-combat story-driven game? Hmm... I guess only time will tell.

It's funny that they mentioned a romantic comedy game. I have a proposal for such a game that I tried shopping around in Leipzig last year. Current adventure publishers have no interest in producing a game of this nature, so it would be ironic if one came out of a company like BioWare first.

We really are living in interesting times that have the potential for great things for the adventure player. However, as always, it's not clear what kind of future is in store for current adventure developers. I hope that we can all play an important part in the genre's development – it IS something we love doing after all.

Interactive Dialogue – An Approach to Structure

(Originally published as The Conversation in Develop Magazine)

With the success of Heavy Rain and the critical acclaim it has so far received, narrative is once again thrust to the forefront of game development. Like casual and social gaming have recently done in their own areas of the gaming spectrum, Heavy Rain has broadened the interactive experience in what has traditionally been regarded as the "hard core" arena. The lines that define what makes a game have been blurred once more, but what might it mean for developers in general and game writers in particular?

If the industry is to embrace stronger, character-driven narrative without abandoning the heart of what makes a great game – solid gameplay – how might we approach it? How can we structure interactive scenes and dialogue in a way to give the player gameplay control without becoming overwhelmed at the writing stage?

The key to a writer of interactive dialogue keeping control of the writing process and feeding into the game's design and development in a constructive way is twofold. Firstly, a writer should learn to think through the structure of interactive scenes in terms of Boolean variables and secondly, they should abandon all thoughts of dialogue trees.

Although I'm aiming this article primarily at game writers, it is also intended for anyone involved in developing the structure of interactive dialogue scenes. Designers, for instance, may not have the job of writing the dialogue in the scenes, but understanding and working with the structure is important, particularly if they are the ones who need to track down and fix bugs later in development.

How much interactive dialogue a game needs or the degree to which it is implemented depends very much on the requirements of the game. This approach to interactive dialogue should always be a part of the overall development with the importance of its role defined by the team's creative leads.

Structure and Boolean Variables

For any writers who may not know what a Boolean variable is – perhaps not having any experience in coding at any level – it is a simple variable that has just two values: True or False. The beauty here is that there is no ambiguity, which enables everything to be kept neat and tidy. But, you may ask, how will this help those writers who never go near scripts that contain variables?

While writers don't need to learn to create logic scripts or step on the development team's toes in this respect, they will find it incredibly helpful to think in this way, not only to keep track of the complex interactions taking place, but also use Booleans as a tool in the creation of the structure.

At the simplest level, the use of Boolean variables can stop multiple characters telling the player character the same piece of information or stop a character repeating dramatic dialogue and diminishing the drama.

One of the problems with developing interactive scenes is that they can quickly become very daunting and may overwhelm writers if they don't have some method of structuring their approach. Yes, be aware of the larger picture, but concentrate on the building blocks themselves in a way that creates that picture.

When approaching any interactive dialogue scene try defining – in terms of Booleans – what the player character knows, what he needs to know, who he has spoken to, what has been discussed, what he has in his inventory and what his goals/objectives are. For example: Has the PC spoken to Mary? Is there a bomb in the inventory? Does the PC have the name of the murder victim?

The dialogue itself will be coloured by story, plot, the agendas of the other characters and whatever sub-plots are taking place, but controlling the information states with Boolean variables will keep the structure manageable. You end up with a lot of variables, but if they are named in ways that make sense it can be easy to track them.

It can be tempting to use variables that increment, but this can cause logic bugs which are difficult to track down and hard to fix. If you had a variable called Bill_Conversation that incremented with each subject discussed, it would only be possible to discuss topics in a specific order or the incrementation and conditional topics will break down and bugs will appear. Forcing a specific order goes against the whole idea of an interactive dialogue scene and it may as well be a cut scene.

Naming variables based on the purpose they serve and the characters or objects to which they relate enables you to manage a list of them much more easily. If we have three characters in a game: Tom (player character), Dick and Harry, we may have variables named:

– Tom_Knows_Banana – he knows he needs a banana.

– Dick_Spoken_Banana – Tom has spoken to Dick about the banana

– Harry_Spoken_Banana – Tom has spoken to Harry about the banana

All these variables will start out as False and Tom cannot speak to Dick or Harry about the banana until he knows he needs to do so.

If Tom, through the actions of the player, finds that he needs a banana, we set the Tom_Knows_Banana variable to True. This in turn means that when the player interacts with Dick, say, we can trigger the part of his interactive scene that's conditional on this variable. When Tom has discussed the banana with Dick we set the Dick_Spoken_Banana variable to True. Not only can we use this to stop Tom and Dick talking about the banana again (unless we specifically want them to), it also acts as an information flag that Tom is effectively carrying around with him from this point on.

If the player interacts with Harry, he and Tom can talk about the banana. Tom and Harry may talk before Tom and Dick, but we'll assume that Tom has already spoken to Dick about the banana before talking to Harry. Tom asks Harry about a banana and he then tells Tom that Dick likes fruit and might have one. Because Tom has already spoken to Dick, the variable Dick_Spoken_Banana is True and triggers a nested condition where Tom explains that he already asked Dick. In scripting terms it may look like this:

```
IF((Tom_Knows_Banana == True) &&
(Harry_Spoken_Banana == False))
```

```
{
    [Ask Harry about the banana. Harry
    says Dick may have one.]
    IF(Dick_Spoken_Banana == True)
    {
    [Tom says he already asked Dick.]
}
    Harry_Spoken_Banana = True;
}
```

Obviously, talking about bananas is a very simple example, but even this can get complex if the number of characters increases or the route to getting the information about the banana has additional gameplay complexity. We may, for instance, introduce another interactive character, Sally, who will only say something important after Tom has spoken to both Dick and Harry. This part of Sally's scene is then dependent on both variables Dick_Spoken_Banana and Harry_Spoken_Banana being set to True.

What you may notice is that although we've potentially created a lot of structure, there is no dialogue. While we establish the structure dialogue is irrelevant – writers can have the fun of creating that at a later stage. In a sense, this has a parallel with the scene creation approach to film scriptwriting, but in terms of game writing it becomes potentially much more complex. A typical film might have around forty scenes but a game may have hundreds.

One particular beauty in this structural approach is that the development team can see the shape that's forming much earlier because they don't have to wait for the dialogue. The gameplay implementation of the interactive scenes can take place before the writer has completed the dialogue, which will likely benefit schedules and milestone targets.

No Dialogue Trees

Some people may think it an absolute necessity to have dialogue trees in order that scenes will be fully interactive, but I find that thinking in terms of dialogue trees is distracting. In seventeen years of developing interactive dialogue scenes I've never used a branching tree structure. I find that the structure I outlined above is far more flexible and enables the writer to think of each discussion topic as a separate building block but linked and perhaps modified by the use of the Boolean variables and what those variables control.

To me it's much clearer when approaching a scene to think of all discussion topics as being at the same level. The availability of the topics is controlled through the script by the Booleans as described above. After discussing a topic the dialogue engine should return back to that same level to enable the player to choose the next topic.

One of the problems of developing dialogue with a tree structure in mind is that there is often the need to copy whole sections of dialogue into new places in the tree in order to get them to trigger in the right way. This strikes me as very clumsy and a huge waste of time. If dialogue needs to be copied and pasted anywhere, then there is likely to be a problem with the scene structure or the system that drives the dialogue.

Further Complexity

There may be times when the "flat" approach to topics will need to deal with a second layer temporarily. The writer may want to give the player choices that have different outcomes and doesn't want to return to the main level and confuse the issue with topics that don't have an immediate bearing. An interrogation, for example, may throw up critical information that the player character concentrates on until the resultant sub-topics have been exhausted.

This second level of topics is not a tree structure and can best be described as a nested level of topics. It should be thought of in the same "flat" way. In scripting terms you might think of it as a kind of "while loop" where the conversation is held in this level until the condition for release is met, at which point the system should return to the original topic level.

Many games will not have a need for the complexity of multiple levels, but if it is required the team needs to ensure it is built into the dialogue system.

Emotions are a further way to add complexity, particularly if the choices the player makes and the actions of the gameplay have an effect on the emotions of the other characters. If the player has done something to make Dick angry with Tom we may set a Dick_Angry variable to True and create conditional dialogue within the interactive scene that is triggered by this variable. It may be, for instance, that Dick refuses to talk about anything at all while he's Angry with Tom, in which case the player may need to discover a way to placate Dick before he can get the information he needs. Or the player may need to discover another way altogether to get that same information.

As mentioned before, how much complexity you need is dictated by the requirements of the game and how important interactive dialogue is to the experience you want to give the player. Take these ideas and adapt them to your needs.

Conclusion

In many ways, approaching the writing of interactive scenes is blurring the boundaries between writing and design, which is not a bad thing. The more they become intertwined the better integrated the story and gameplay will be. The two aspects will marry closely and share a clear vision.

Because Boolean variables can only be True or False, it may seem that there is a danger of losing the spectrum of subtlety. They are not there to define the subtlety, or the lack of such, but control the structure within which the team creates the subtlety. The use of multiple Booleans working together will create its own subtlety, of course, but the real subtlety will always come from the writer knowing the characters well and knowing how they will react to being teased, seduced, interrogated, etc.

The interactive structure is not a substitute for good writing, but a tool that enables the writer and designers to make it work in the best possible way for the player.

Designing Puzzles Backwards

(Originally published in 2 parts on
gamedesignaspect.blogspot.com)

I've spent most of my game development career working on various story-based games; mostly traditional adventures but other types, too. Although there are different kinds of puzzles involved in the creation of such a game, the kind I find most satisfying are the ones that tie the gameplay directly into the story by the means of shared objectives.

When I'm fortunate to have the opportunity to create both the story and design of a game, as I did with *So Blonde*, for instance, I like to work in a very iterative manner. I get the basic structure of the story sorted before working up some detail, which then allows me to start defining the gameplay objectives based upon that story, which then feeds back into the developing plot. By working this way, the plot becomes a high level structure that gives both the gameplay and story the shape it needs and enables me to start working up the puzzle details.

When I'm in a position to work on an objective related puzzle, I find it's best to start with the objective and work backwards. By taking this approach I ensure that each step of the puzzle – or other gameplay that feeds into the puzzle – links to the objective in a clear way.

As I work on such puzzles I loosely go through a series of questions that help with the process.

- What is the objective?

- What is stopping the player character from reaching that objective?
- How will the player deal with that blockage?
- How will the player get the items/skills needed to do so?
- Are there separate or side objectives the player has to deal with in order to get what's required?
- How can I make this more complex?
- How can I make this more fun?
- Is this series of events logical?
- Is it clear to the player what they need to achieve and what they need to do to achieve it?

There may be plenty more questions relating to the specifics of a puzzle or the objects used and even the user interface, but the main thing to remember is that if you're not asking yourself these kinds of questions, you've got to ask yourself why not.

During my time at Revolution Software I was fortunate to work with some talented people and much of what I learned about developing and refining of puzzles comes from that period. When we developed the second Broken Sword game, The Smoking Mirror, the designers came up with one of my favourite puzzles (I was actually producer on that title).

The player character, George, arrives at the Marseilles docks at night and needs to find a specific warehouse. Unfortunately, there is a fence barring his way. The objective here is to get over that fence – it's clear what the player needs to do and only by getting over the fence can the story progress.

Now we know the player character's objective, how do we stop him from simply climbing over the fence? (We've started asking the questions.) A vicious dog is placed at the other side of the fence which makes its intentions clear as soon as the player interacts with the fence.

How will the player deal with the dog? It needs to be distracted in some way.

What can we use to distract the dog? There are biscuits inside the hut.

How do we make this more complex? There's also a man inside the hut and the door to the hut is on the other side of the fence.

We now have two additional sub-objectives to complete that feed into the main objective of distracting the dog to climb the fence – the player must distract the man and find a way into the hut to get the biscuits.

Of course, it's possible for George to talk to the guy in the hut, but although the conversation is fun and somewhat informative, it's not the solution to this puzzle. What the conversation does, though, is to give the player logical options to try. If the player sees a guy in a hut it's natural to tap on the window and have a chat.

As the details of the puzzle were expanded, not only did they add to the richness of the puzzle, they also helped define the geography of the location. For instance, the need for a trapdoor in the floor of the hut meant that we needed the player character to be able to get to the area beneath the hut without this giving a means to get to the other side of the fence. Anyone interested in learning further details may like to play the game for themselves. :)

It may seem to make sense that, when working backwards in this way, you continue the process until you reach the previous objective conclusion. However, this only works if the game is completely linear.

It may be that you need to work backwards until you reach the point the player finds out what this objective is. During gameplay, reaching the previous objective could give the information to player about this objective, but there might be other ways the player gets such information. Half way towards an objective the player may discover information that gives him additional objectives that will now run in parallel to the current one.

With multiple objectives, working backwards must end up with the same starting point for each, which can be a good check that the puzzles are sound.

Like anything else used in the development of a game design, working backwards in this way is just a tool as part of a whole range. No matter how well used this tool is, it isn't a complete solution.

The ultimate test of this kind of puzzle is to think it through forwards as if playing the game in your head, looking for potential problems, logic flaws, lack of clarity and ways to refine the steps of the puzzle.

Design it backwards, think it through forwards. Reiterate.

5 Things Screenwriters Can Learn From Games

(Originally published on bang2write.com)

I was recently at a conference in Rio when someone posed the following: *"People say that film is a director's medium and TV is a producer's medium – whose medium is games?"*

I'd never been asked this before but my answer was almost immediate – *"Games are the player's medium."*

Because they're such an important part of developing games and interactive stories, players must be seen as both participators and the audience.

By thinking about how the player is considered during the development of game narratives, screenwriters can learn a number of key points.

1. Game Writers are Players

It's almost impossible to write for games if you don't play and understand them, not just in terms of how they should be played, but knowing why a game is fun and rewarding to play. Because there are so many thousands of games out there and so little time, it's not possible to play all games and it's unlikely that any of us will enjoy all types of games, but a game writer who gets a buzz out of playing games, particularly narrative games, will understand the role of the player in the writing and development process. Being players gives game writers the right insights into their craft.

In parallel, screenwriters must be viewers who enjoy watching TV shows or films and understand what make them enjoyable to their audience. They must understand why structure is the way it is, how pacing affects the feel of the story, how the filming and the actors fit into the process and many other aspects of the craft.

KEY POINT 1 – Just as game writers must play games, screenwriters must be regular viewers of their medium.

2. We Write for an Audience of One

When we write our game narratives we are writing for an audience of one, no matter how many copies of a game is sold. The individual player, with his or her hands on the controller, is our audience. This even applies to a massively multiplayer game because it's only ever that one player who's making their own interactive choices. No one else is selecting those choices for them.

Although the viewers of a film or TV show are not interacting with the media to make the story progress, the individual is still immensely important, even in a cinema filled with people or amongst a family sitting at home. Screenwriters must still write in a way that connects to the individual or they will not feel the empathy you need. Also, with an increasing number of ways for individuals to access and view various media, they are regularly watched by people on their own.

KEY POINT 2 – Games teach us that the individual audience member is highly important.

3. The Player is the Protagonist

This applies whether you write first person or third person games. The story doesn't move forward without the actions of the player, which gives the player a protagonist's connectivity to the twists and turns of the plot, the conflict with other characters and the motivation to overcome obstacles along the way. Yes, the stories and choices may well be pre-defined, written and recorded, but done well the suspension of disbelief will encourage the player to believe they are saving the world or solving the murder mystery.

It's very easy to think of film and TV as passive media because viewers are not interacting with the story, but passive implies a lack of engagement and that's definitely not the case. Viewers engage very strongly and while the media may be non-interactive and viewer is not the protagonist, screenwriters should ensure that the engagement is maximised by creating characters with which the viewer can identify.

KEY POINT 3 – Games are highly interactive but that doesn't mean film or TV is passive.

4. We Write Characters the Player Will Want to Play

Lara Croft or Master Chief didn't get to be popular game characters by accident – they were created and written with the player in mind. The very best characters you could ever come up with might count for nothing if they are not fun to play. Admittedly, you might argue that good, playable characters fall into the realm of game design, but if you want the story to connect to the gameplay in a cohesive manner, the writing and design must overlap throughout the whole development process, particularly with design.

Similarly, screenwriters must write characters the viewer will want to watch. Without these great characters on the page, the directors and actors can't begin to visualise the ideas you want to put across and the viewers, should the script get made, would struggle to engage.

KEY POINT 4 – Game players love to engage with great characters; your viewers do, too.

5. We Create Stories and Worlds in which the Player Feels Alive

The game worlds aren't there simply for the characters to exist within, they are worlds in which the player enjoys the combat or investigating or solving puzzles. The stories support and enhance this and give a richer experience to the player. Equally, the player must feel that the world has a consistency that makes sense in relation to the story and the gameplay. No one wants a surprise thrust upon them that kills them unfairly or expects them to solve a puzzle when it relies on a mechanic you didn't even know existed. The same goes for the stories and worlds you create – be as unusual as you like but deliver a consistency that enables the player to feel like a vibrant part of your world.

In a comparable fashion, the story worlds you create for your screenplays should support the characters and ideas in a way that's believable and doesn't interrupt the suspension of disbelief. Sometimes the worlds need to be big and bold like your ideas, but other times they can be much simpler because they help the ideas by giving them a clearer focus. Having the characters fit within these worlds is an important part of engaging the viewer.

KEY POINT 5 – A game's world supports and enhances its characters. Your screenplays should have worlds that do the same.

Ultimately, games cannot tell you how to write your screenplay, but by studying these parallels – and any others you may find – the different perspective can help you hone your skills by making you question the creative process.

Understanding the player/viewer role is an important part of placing yourself into that person's mind.

Her Story is not Your Story

(Originally published on gamedeveloper.com)

And as much as I love the game and wish I'd written it, it's not My Story, either.

I've written this article in response to one by *Christian Donlan on Eurogamer*, which I think is wonderful. I'd like to thank Christian for providing such great food for thought.

In particular, this line made me pause: "it's not Her Story but Your Story as you weigh the evidence and apportion motives as you see fit."

I understand and appreciate his reasoning and it's hard not to agree, but I'd like to put forward a different outlook on the subject by looking at Her Story and the larger question of to whom the story belongs in a game.

Her Story is not your story. Piecing it together is your experience and how it shapes in your mind is unique to you, but that doesn't make it your story.

The pieces fit together as a kind of jigsaw – the time stamps on the clips help with this. The way you uncover things and the emphasis the pieces have in the picture you are putting together is a little malleable so certain pieces will have greater significance than others because of that personal unveiling.

This is similar to watching a TV series out of order – you'd still arrange it in your mind the correct way, but how it colours your view of the story will be different to the way it might have been if you'd watched the episodes in the intended order. You may not enjoy it as much because some of the impact of storytelling is in the way we create setup and payoff and a different viewing order may undermine that.

Episodes 1–3 of Star Wars had a problem that was too large to surmount in this respect – we'd already had the payoff of who Darth Vader was so it was hard to care about Anakin Skywalker.

The revealing of the narrative in Her Story is kind of like watching Memento – the pieces of Shelby's story are presented to us in an unconventional order and the true shape of it falls into place at the end. The difference in Her Story is that instead of the writer/director choosing the order in which the fragments are presented, the player uncovers them through the keywords he or she chooses.

With Her Story, the interview pieces have implied conflict, but they also constantly pose questions about the interviewee, her situation, the people around her and even the story she's telling. She isn't addressing the player, she's addressing the people who are interviewing her. We feel that we are viewing something that genuinely happened.

One of the things I particularly like is that the video snippets don't sound like monologues. Too many games suffer from the problem that talking with characters feels like you're triggering brief monologues. Even diary entries feel like this. More so, really. Games that rely on diary entries and notes for the player so often leave me cold because it's too obviously a game design thing rather than a story thing. They are written specifically for the player and seem, at times, to bypass the character we are playing.

I've always been a firm believer of taking the player into account when developing a game and most developers do this very well where the game's mechanics and interface go. Where they often fall down is in how they bear in mind the way the player thinks when dealing with the story, characters, dialogue and the interaction with those things. Her Story is excellent in the way it handles this because the whole game is about how the player thinks while revealing the story and gives the player a great bond with the narrative. For me, it is the best connection to a game's story I've ever felt. (The only better link to an interactive story was the second episode of TryLife, but that's not really a game, although I highly recommend it.)

What I particularly liked is the way that, although we never hear the voice of the interviewer, the interviewee's responses tell us what was asked and we build up an implied picture of the person asking the questions.

Now I've swayed back and forth a few times on whether Her Story is actually a game or not, but after asking myself a lot of questions I'm firmly of the opinion that this IS a game. A game in which there is one big puzzle we must solve through the way we interact with this incredibly simple interface and view a fixed set of video clips.

However, this isn't a game that responds to our probing by giving different scenarios or to branch the narrative towards a different ending. This is a game in which WE respond to the unfolding of the narrative – it's about how we react to a fixed narrative based upon how we're able to view it and the order in which it's revealed.

One thing that struck me when comparing Christian's article to my own thoughts was that developers and game critics have become obsessed with the player's narrative. This is where the bigger question of whose story it actually is really comes into play.

I think we need to differentiate between experience and narrative – just because you experience something in a way that's unique to you, it doesn't make that your narrative. When I walk down the street on a beautiful day, it's not a narrative, no matter how much I enjoyed the experience.

If I view an abstract painting in a gallery and admire the way the artist has used colour, shape and texture to create an intriguing piece and I then see a face in the work that the artist didn't intend, the painting isn't suddenly mine. The experience of my interpretation of the artist's work is uniquely mine and no one can take that away, but the artist placed those brush strokes in a specific way and nothing has changed that. The painting is still its own thing.

In a similar way, this is true of all those games with branching narratives – all the elements have been created and every possible path through the story already exists. The player is not creating a new story, simply unfolding a pre-defined one. It may well be that the one you experience is different to the one your friend unfolded, but how can it be yours when the creators already defined it?

Her Story is slightly different in this respect, because the interpretation of the existing story in the player's mind is a fundamental part of the whole experience. This is what separates it from every other game. Okay, that's a sweeping statement because I haven't played every other game by a long way, but it's still not your story. It's not the player's story.

It's also not the creator's story.

We should always remember that a good narrative is about the characters – it is the characters' story and regardless of how the story unfolds it is about those characters. When Christian Bale played Batman for three films, the stories within them didn't become Bale's stories, they were Batman's stories.

The beauty of games is that, instead of just watching other people play these great roles and become these fantastic characters on screen, players step onto the stage themselves and play these important roles. The player is incredibly vital to moving the story forward because they have taken on the part of the main character, generally without rehearsal, which means having to learn the role as they go. This is, of course, a strong part of the experience – learning the character you are attempting to play. The player shares the character's story and drives the progression through it.

Even in a first person game, the player knows that they are playing a role in which they are the hero fighting aliens or zombies, say, or exploring a haunted house or a deadly dungeon. The player takes on the role of the character directly.

A third person game may distance us a little from the role or give us the opportunity to take on multiple roles as the game switches the playable character, but we still identify closely with the character we are playing.

Without players understanding that they are taking on the roles of these characters, we would never be able to switch from one game to another as easily as we do and the characters in them, moving from Gordon Freeman to Batman to Lara Croft to the Traveller (Journey) for instance.

In Her Story, the player doesn't take on the role of the character being interviewed or even the interviewer. Instead we become a nameless researcher looking into the case through a database of stored interview clips that can only be accessed through the use of keyword searches. Admittedly, that doesn't take too much scrutiny or we are in danger of seeing this role as "the player" and may lose our connection to the story we're trying to discover. Suspension of disbelief is an important factor here.

I think that Sam Barlow has been very clever in manipulating our interpretations of the story he created. We've already had our ideas coloured by the trailer he created, before we even started to play the game, but the way that he's cut up the videos into very specific snippets is very manipulative, too. Are we genuinely interpreting this story in a way that's unique to us or are we being manipulated into a very specific interpretation? Either way, it's a very clever idea, brilliantly crafted and one that will make me think deeply about game stories for some time to come.

This isn't Your Story but Her Story. At best, it's Your Interpretation of Her Story. But really, I think it's Your Interpretation of Her Story as Influenced by the Manipulations of Sam Barlow.

And, considering how much like a genuine experience he's made the whole thing feel, I find this wonderful. I hope it means that we'll all be inspired by it.

Adventure Games and Me

(originally published on Adventure-Treff.de)

I often think about my relationship with adventure games.

I'm so busy with my writing and other interests that my time for playing games, including adventures, has become virtually non-existent. I feel slightly disconnected from the genre as a whole and, in many respects, from the people who make and love adventures, which is more than a little embarrassing as so many of these people I like to think of as my friends.

Does that make me a poor friend? Maybe.

Does that make me a bad adventure developer? Possibly.

Does it mean I no longer love adventures? Definitely not!

Being involved in the writing and design of an adventure is one of the most enjoyable things to do.

The adventure game, when done well, is the perfect melding of story, character and gameplay. The genre has the potential to explore virtually any narrative theme in a way that requires the player to advance the story through gameplay. The type of gameplay makes it impossible to bolt on a story as an afterthought or to write dialogue without knowing the complete sweep of the story and gameplay.

Richard Dansky recently wrote, "The most important thing to look for in a game writer is a game writer. Everything else is secondary." This applies especially to adventures and the most important thing to look for in an adventure writer is the ability to write adventure games.

Such a statement may seem a little self-serving, but probably more than in any other genre, a writer of adventures should ideally be a game designer, too, with a particular understanding of the needs of the adventure game. It's almost impossible to separate writing from design in this genre. At the very least, a writer must work so closely with a designer that the process they go through would appear to be undertaken by a single person. Without the tight knitting together of writing and design the cracks between the two will begin to show.

However, it's rarely a simple or straightforward task. I've worked with writers from other disciplines who, although they've worked on a number of games, still have to be reminded that a particular character can't do something specific automatically because it should happen through the actions of the player. I even have to remind myself of such things from time to time. Often, the old ways of storytelling have to be unlearned and re-learned in a different, player-focused way.

If you write prose fiction (short stories, novels) you should think about how the words you write bring the world and characters alive within the readers' imaginations. If you write a film script you ought to have a sense of how that screenplay will look and feel when turned into a film and projected onto the big screen. If you cannot do these things, how do you know your novel or film script will work?

When writing a game, not only do you need to visualise how it will work on screen (often in multiple platform formats), you must do so with the player's anticipated presence guiding every part of the creative process.

An adventure game writer must imagine the experience of the game during the creation process as if they're playing it on behalf of the player and long before any assets are created that will see the story and gameplay come to life. Even from a very high level, where gameplay only exists as objectives and loose ideas, a sense of how it will play out and how the characters relate to one-another will help when drilling down into the details for the final story and design.

Some game writers feel they don't need to know game design, but it's like a film writer not understanding the way a film is shot, how the actors will portray the characters and how the director fits into the process. Even if a game writer doesn't want to actually create the detailed gameplay, they should still have an understanding of how a game is designed so they can work more closely with the team to ensure that story, characters and dialogue are in synch with the gameplay.

The strength of a writer-designer is that they are able to think through the way the player will have to find object A, combine it with object B and use it on hole C. How does this puzzle fit with the style of the game world and the characters? What kind of wry/sarcastic/humorous comment will the player character make at each stage? How do we keep the player interested? Are we providing enough challenge without making the game too difficult? Is there a cohesion that gives the game a holistic feel?

And it's that holistic feel I love about adventures and it's why I enjoy creating adventures so much. How the story, plot, characters and dialogue all support and enrich the gameplay. I love, too, the way I have to constantly develop a number of disciplines in order to regularly deliver story-designs that I'm happy with.

I hope, too, that those stories and designs are ones players enjoy. It's always a pleasure to meet players at events like Gamescom and talk to them about adventure games (and other things, too, of course). Almost without exception, I've found the adventure players I've met to be warm, friendly people that I have a lot of respect for and who are a pleasure to talk with. Knowing that I'm creating for a genre you enjoy is a delight itself, in addition to my simple love of creating.

I once had a discussion with a work colleague in which I said I loved creating games far more than I loved playing them, which he didn't feel was right. But that's how I am – my creative urges are so great that I must constantly feed them and writing and designing adventures are a great way to do just that.

So, while I think that the adventure will mature and evolve over the coming years, I hope it continues to inspire me to work in the genre for a long time to come.

Rules for Game Writing?

(Originally published on my blog)

There was a wonderful article on the Guardian website: Ten Rules for Writing Fiction. It's two pages are filled with lots of writers' rules and tips and I'm sure it's a good read for writers at all stages of their careers.

I started thinking about the possibility of coming up with my own set of rules specifically aimed at game writing and after thinking about it for a little time my initial thought was that it might not be possible to do this at all.

My reason for thinking this was that I looked at the idea from the same position as these fiction writers – they are listing these rules, on the whole, as advice to novice or inexperienced writers. A common "theme" is advice on writing regularly and keeping up the writing. As a would be writer of novels, a novice would be expected to complete a novel before sending it off to agents and/or publishers. Similarly with plays or film scripts – the writer tends to complete the work before sending it out to those who are potential buyers.

With game writing the role of the writer is very different. Very rarely, if ever, does a writer create a script for a game and send it to developers and publishers. How would a developer know that this great story and dialogue will make a great game? Unless the writer is also a game designer – creating a 500+ page design document that includes the story and dialogue – the writer will not make it into games this way. Developers tend to have more than enough of their own ideas to consider outside stories and publishers will only consider signing up a project if it already has a development team attached to it. Far more often than not, a writer will join a team on a project that's already in development. Hopefully, early enough in the development process that you can make the story and characters your own, so to speak.

Of course, it's perfectly possible to team up with a development studio and create a game pitch as a joint venture. I'm currently in this process with a kids' game idea I had, but this is much more a game design thing than a writing thing (though I will be writing as well). In such a case, you have to convince the developer that your idea has legs, but before approaching publishers you need to create the pitch documents, game design ideas, story synopsis, character gameplay abilities, etc. You and the team would have to think about the size of the project, the workload it would need and the budget that it's likely to require to bring to market. Now you're doing ten things you didn't expect because you only wanted to write for games. Blimey!

With this in mind, and before this turns into a long essay on game design and production, I'm going to attempt to write some rules for game writing. Or should that be Rules for the Game Writer?

0. Gameplay comes first

Actually, it's so important, it's more important than first. Without gameplay, there would be no game. When we get wrapped up in our great story ideas or cool dialogue, it can be easy to forget this, but everything you create as a writer should be done to enhance the gameplay experience. It's also important to understand the gameplay style of the game you're working on and ensure that what you do is in keeping with this style.

1. Be prepared for a lot of hard work

Writing is hard work. Game writing can be a lot harder. Much of this is down to the sheer volume of dialogue needed for some types of games. A typical film has 1000 to 1100 lines of dialogue, but for many game this is no big deal. A 12,000 to 20,000 line total is very common and some games can have 40,000 lines or more.

2. Work well with others

If a game has 20,000 lines, it's unlikely that a single writer will be given the task of writing so much story and dialogue - it's the equivalent of writing about 20 feature films. This means that you may be one of a team of writers working on a game and so you need to be a part of that team in a constructive way.

You'll also be part of the bigger development team and may well find yourself working with designers, artists, animators, etc as you all work towards a consistent vision.

3. Learn game design

You don't have to become a game designer, but having an understanding of at least the rudimentary principles will go a long way. Not only will it give you better insights into the development process, you will see how certain story and character aspects will and won't work within the concept of the game. It will save you a lot of time in re-writes if you can foresee gameplay related story problems before they occur and you hand in the story overview. Game design doesn't have to be difficult – just get yourself Game Maker from Yoyo Games; it's not expensive (there's even a free version).

4. Accept changes

There will always be the need to make changes. Mostly it's down to things outside of your control – publisher feedback, testing feedback, design changes, etc. Whatever the reason, make the changes work in a positive way. Sometimes it may seem that a change is being made for the sake of it and you may feel justified in defending your ideas against the change. If you feel it's something important, then it's right that you do so, but learn to realise when you're fighting a losing battle and back down with grace and move on.

5. Play games

And play a variety of games. It's not enough to play Farmville or World of Warcraft for twenty hours a week.

6. Read the gaming press and fan forums

Read a broad cross-section to avoid bias. Read what kind of things fans are saying, particularly about games in the same style as the one you're working on. If you read online comments about your own work, be prepared for some harsh words, deserved or otherwise.

7. Do other things

Live a life outside of your game writing life. Not only will this keep you sane, you get a much broader, balanced outlook that can feed into your writing.

8. Travel by bus

With your headphones off. Listen to how natural conversations work - the to-and-fro, the interruptions, the overlaps. Treat every such opportunity (the train, the coffee shop, etc.) as food for your creative mind.

9. Play a musical instrument

Or any other type of hobby that's not writing. I'm teaching myself to play the bass guitar as a fun distraction. I doubt that I'll ever join a band (a bit too long in the tooth for that) but who cares? It's a fun thing to do. Swim, hike, do the gardening - whatever you want.

I hope some of that works for you.

Game Writing for Young People

(Originally published on writing.ie)

Engaging young people in any kind of writing can be a challenge to parents, teachers and even the youngsters themselves. The modern world and the range of interests for many of them do not naturally lead to an interest in the written word.

Games like Minecraft, however, show us that huge numbers of children are interested in creating whole worlds and sharing them with friends. It therefore doesn't take an enormous leap to conclude that game writing and interactive storytelling is likely to engage many young people.

Most kids love playing games and many of those would really enjoy making their own, but beginning the process can seem like a hugely daunting task. Yet it doesn't need to be and from my own experience of running workshops in schools (as well as for other age groups) I know that children of all abilities connect with interactive storytelling very quickly.

We all love telling stories in one form or another and game writing is another type that adds to the range. With my three decades in the games industry and my experience of giving talks and workshops across the world, I know that young people (and those not so young) find the interactive approach to storytelling refreshing and inspiring.

Of course, interactive stories are not limited to games. Stories like those in the old "choose your own adventure" books were hugely popular in the 1980s and are even making a comeback now. People are using interactivity to explore storytelling in the mediums of TV and films with great success (*Bandersnatch* and *TryLife*, for example). So understanding these ways of telling stories at any age, not only gives a person insights they may not have had before, but can also lead to new avenues of creativity they had not previously considered.

Game writing is a fascinating way of using narrative and one that gets the mind firing on many levels. The writer of interactive stories has to be both creative and logical and learn how to balance the two in the process of telling great tales.

"How," you may ask, "do I even begin to learn this way of writing? It can't be that easy." Yet it isn't particularly difficult if you approach it in the right manner, which is why I enjoy sharing my knowledge with others through workshops I run. These sessions became the basis for my new book, *An Introduction to Game Writing*, which takes the reader through a clear, step-by-step process in a very hands-on way.

Working through the book will have you, your children, grandchildren, nephews, nieces, friends, students and anyone else you know, creating interactive stories in a very short space of time.

One of the main reasons I wanted to create this book specifically was that no one has so far released a game writing book for a younger audience. There are plenty of volumes on the subject aimed at already experienced writers or advanced students, but enriching younger people's creativity is something we should all aim for if we can.

Kids are incredibly smart and have fabulous imaginations but need a variety of ways to express themselves and, hopefully, have fun doing so. While it's good to teach children how to create interactive stories, they also need to be encouraged to do so in their own way and explore outside of the process. These young storytellers will be creating the entertainment of the future and hopefully they will be doing so in ways that excite and surprise us.

Young people are not the only ones who should learn game writing. With an understanding of the subject, you could gain valuable insights into your own writing, which can only ever be a good thing. Reading articles and books on writing can be rewarding from the perspectives they give and a knowledge of interactivity in telling tales will likely help you, too. At the very least you may finally understand what your young relatives see in all the games they play.

Although the book puts no emphasis on spelling and grammar, I do believe in the importance of these, along with other related matters. Teachers can therefore use the book in conjunction with other lessons to hopefully give the students a more fulfilling learning experience.

While the book is not designed to turn people into instant game writers, it is a valuable introduction to the subject and the writer who becomes fired up by the ideas it contains will surely find their own multiple paths into the rich forest of interactive narrative possibilities.

You may think this isn't for you or the kids you know, but consider this: choosing to learn something new is interactive itself. "Do I really want to learn this?"

If you choose No: Move on with your life but worry that you may regret the choice for the rest of your days.

If you choose Yes: Celebrate the fact that you will be learning new skills and keeping your mind fresh.

Game writing is about writing with the player's choices in mind but also about exploring new ways of telling stories with an interactive slant.

Part 2
Developing
Thoughts

(A regular column that was originally published on Randomville)

Oh Lucky Man...

I've recently had cause to look back over the last eleven years of my life and take stock. Often when you embark on such a reflective journey the gems and turds you discover along the way surprise you. Fortunately for me, my introspection turned up far more gems than turds and for this I consider myself a very lucky individual. For instance, how many people get given their chance on the say-so of a talented comic artist of the calibre of Dave Gibbons? Or to work on a day to day basis with a gaming luminary such as Charles Cecil?

I must admit to bluffing my way through those first few weeks in the job. I knew next to nothing about computers, and less than nothing when it came to creating and editing graphics on one of the damn beasts. But I've always been a quick learner and this, along with the support and understanding of other talented individuals in the team, enabled me to pull through. It wasn't long before the feeling I was going to be rumbled began to recede. From such a humble beginning it's been an uphill road the whole way, due to the constantly shifting goalposts of the gaming market, but the satisfaction I've derived from it has more than kept pace.

One of the most gratifying aspects of my time in development has been the chance to meet and to work with so many talented individuals – programmers, artists, animators, musicians, designers, writers, directors, producers, and testers.

People who have made my work much easier. People who have helped catalyse brainstorming sessions to the point where an electric charge fills the air. People who have put in long hours of very hard work in order to add the polish prior to immovable deadlines. People I have a great deal of respect and admiration for.

My eleven years have seen a lot of exciting changes in the way that games are developed and the way they are presented to the player. What was once seen as sophisticated at a screen resolution of 320×200, is now relegated to the realms of the retro section at the back of many gaming magazines. Where once a team of eight completed a game, a top-flight game will now pull in the talents of forty, fifty, sixty or more people. From counting the number of 2D sprites a game would put on screen, we now measure the number of 3D polygons and texture memory a game is able to wring out of state-of-the-art graphics cards.

For me, the most exciting time in game development is still to come, in the area of my own field of expertise – writing and design. Long gone is the time when a superficial story would do and the quality of translations didn't matter too much. Now we endeavour to tell a story through dynamic dialogue that would be at home in the best Hollywood films and ensure that the translated versions are equally powerful.

With such exciting challenges still ahead of me, is there any wonder I consider myself so lucky?

A Penny for Your Thoughts

While thinking of a way to open this piece, I pondered on the number of times I've read of writers proclaiming that, on meeting readers, the first thing they are asked is, "where do you get your ideas". Now this only happened to me for the first time recently, so it's not something I particularly gave a lot of thought to, until now.

To be honest, I have no idea where my ideas originate, or why they pop into my head at the most inappropriate moments. For those who know me, the glazing over of my eyes mid-way through a conversation, is not because the subject holds no interest, but that an idea has suddenly given birth to itself and is demanding my time in its need to be fed and nurtured. Can I help if my little babies need all the love and attention I can lavish upon them? Would you expect me to cast them out into a cruel world at the height of the blizzard?

Of course, many of my ideas are weak or malformed. Even with the greatest will and attention, they will not survive much beyond the birth process. These are the ideas that no one sees; the ones I forget almost instantly. But for every ten of these poor creatures, there is one that's worth making a mental note of, scribbling down on a piece of paper, or placing in the ideas file on my computer. These are thoughts deserving of serious consideration.

Yet, even then, not all of these ideas are great ones. If twenty percent of them turn out to have any genuine value, I would consider that to be a good result. It is much better to have twenty ideas and throw sixteen away, than to only have only four ideas to begin with. The likelihood of each of those four ideas being a winner is very small. By my twenty percent estimation, you'd be fortunate if one of those ideas bore fruit. Unless, of course, you happen to be a unique individual whose every idea is a gem.

The hardest thing in dealing with ideas is discarding them. There are times when a person has to accept that even the best idea won't work and must push it to one side – the context may be wrong, or it conflicts with the style of the project. If it's a genuinely good idea, they always keep it on file, hopefully to be used in another project. But a person should be prepared to discard the idea and move on – ignoring the pleadings of their babies.

Because the creation of games is built on originality, ideas are a valuable commodity, particularly to those who struggle to come up with ideas themselves. Where would the industry be without the people to originate the ideas? A game needs more than a single gameplay mechanic to succeed in the current market. A couple of one-dimensional characters are not enough to give a game depth. And if it hadn't been for the wealth of technical ideas that have abounded over the years, we would not have the high standards we have come to expect from our games.

A penny? Thoughts appear highly under-valued.

Getting the ball rolling

When starting out on the process of making a game, the initial concept – the project vision – is vitally important to get right, whether you're developing your first game or your tenth. If the direction is not clear from the outset, then the more likely it is that the project will drift aimlessly and require more work than necessary to pull it back on course later.

The initial concept may start from a single idea, but in order to approach publishers or to give clear direction to the project's team, it has to be expanded into a fully realised vision document. Until this is done to a satisfactory level, the project will be going nowhere.

It's likely that a few people will be involved in working towards defining the initial concept, but the majority of staff on the project will not be brought on board until the document states everything that the project aims to do. This should cover the game genre, the intended art style, the technical advances, the unique selling points, a brief story synopsis, and anything else that is deemed necessary to paint the right picture.

Although the document should be a brief, high-level statement of the project's aims, it is still a very difficult one to create and not one to be taken lightly. In many respects it's the most important document that the team will undertake, for it defines the flavour of the rest of the development. It must read well and lay everything out in a manner that means others in the company understand the aims and buy into the vision it portrays.

One of the most difficult hurdles to overcome when dealing with an important document like this is coherence. Part of the process of developing the vision will often entail brainstorming, where a number of people will throw a great variety of ideas into the mix. The intention being that the concept becomes one that is rich with diversity. If there is a lack of cohesion when pulling these ideas together, this will show in the final vision document and any readers may well be left with a feeling that there is something lacking. Each idea and suggestion has to be examined and questioned to determine if they add to the vision in a cohesive way, or simply feel bolted on and out of place.

Very occasionally, this examination will lead to the initial idea being removed or modified in favour of a combination of ideas that give a greater cohesion to the vision. While that may feel a little like throwing the baby out with the bath water, if the result is something better the project is going to benefit greatly as a result. For instance, when the first work began on the game In Cold Blood, the intention was for it to be the third in the Broken Sword series. It quickly became clear that it wasn't a Broken Sword game and so a new hero was born and a great game produced; one that could have felt very forced and artificial, had this been ignored.

The key to success in creating the vision for a game is to be as objective as possible when analysing the overall structure of the document. Only then will you ensure you have a vision that hangs together well.

Taking the Rough with the Smooth

When Revolution released In Cold Blood, after working on it for nearly three years, one of the first magazines to review it gave it only four out of ten. I remember being quite shocked that this thing of beauty, this long labour of love, was not being adored by everyone who played it. What were these people thinking? Did they not realise how much sweat and sleepless nights went into the making of this game?

When you do anything that involves putting your soul on display for everyone to see, there will always be times when some of those people will brandish the whip of harsh criticism as they pass by. Taking your chances in game development's creative free-for-all, means there are times when you've got to be prepared for any ensuing pain.

Of course, there are those of a masochistic nature who revel in the barbed comments that come their way, and others who use it as ammunition to condemn the masses as ignorant plebs, for not finding everything they create to be of sublime merit. But the majority learns to take it in their stride or run the risk of becoming a casualty of criticism.

Personally, I enjoy constructive feedback. In fact, this edition of the column was inspired by an e-mail I received offering some thoughts on my writing. This guy was clever – by starting with compliments on my work in general, he was then able to sneak in some pretty insightful remarks that got me thinking. How evil is that? To get a writer thinking about his own work. And on a weekend, too! If only all criticism was so fair.

Fairness, after all, is the only thing we should hope for when being reviewed or criticised. We have no right to expect kind words or high scores, even when we know it is the best work we could possibly have done; for every person has their own subjective viewpoint which will colour how they approach the material under review.

It is incredibly hard, however, not to feel frustrated by people who write off a game without even seeing it; who seem to think that no one has a right to experiment in a genre that was once renowned for its innovative development. To me, this not only lacks any semblance of fairness, it is also not really criticism – constructive or otherwise.

Whatever the tone of real criticism, I always find that the positive aspects outweigh the negative by a long way. Yes, take on board what is being said in the averse pieces and learn from them if you can; but use the positive to drive you forward with a will that enables you to deal with the negative and make your next project better still.

I once had a guy come up to me in a supermarket and point at the Beneath a Steel Sky T-shirt I wore. "That's the best game I ever played! You should convert the Broken Sword games for the Amiga!"

I welcome your constructive feedback, for I want to give you games, in return, that instil those kinds of responses in people.

Let me tell you a story...

At school one year, when I was about eleven, we used to have one hour each week put aside for writing stories. It was always the final hour before lunch every Wednesday and I would look forward to that part of the week like no other. No thoughts of fame or money drove me, I simply loved to write stories and it's been a passion that's burned within me ever since.

We all love to be told stories; particularly ones that capture our attention and make us hang on the very words of the teller, whatever the medium. A good story, told well, will transport us to new worlds, to new situations that we could never experience for ourselves. It will allow us to see into the mind of an evil antagonist and empathise with the most downtrodden of heroes as the plot unfolds.

The principles behind the construction of stories has been with us for thousands of years, ranging from tales of Greek Gods to epic mediaeval poems; from heart-rending romance to futuristic high adventure. Many fundamentals have stayed with us through that time, yet many more subtleties and sophisticated variations have been developed to allow the act of storytelling to remain fresh and relevant.

Though it is in the field of video games that story faces its biggest single upheaval, as challenges arise to tell stories in ways that adhere to the many established frameworks, but do so in an interactive manner also. Not only must the story be revealed by the actions of the player, it must respond to those same actions in some degree or other.

Games will develop stories that serve different purposes, depending on the requirements of the genre and the degree to which each particular game stresses the importance of the varying possibilities. Is the story, for instance, one with a linear plot that takes the player from the start to the end through a series of connected set-ups and scenarios? Or is it one that ends in the same place, but allows the player to choose the order based on parallel plot threads? Do the actions of the player lead to plot consequences that change the story ending, and so tell a different tale to the one that would have been revealed had the player taken a different course through the game? Or will it be a completely open-ended story; one that is, effectively written by the actions of the player?

Clearly, the next few years, decades even, will be an exciting time, as more variations and complexities arise from the need to tell stories in an increasingly interactive manner. But it will also be a time fraught with frustration and confusion, for we must define the new story-telling rules that will help us speak a common vocabulary.

Many books already exist which cover the telling of stories in other media – film, TV, novels, plays, etc. – but we're only now beginning to scratch the surface of what constitutes telling interactive stories. There has already been some tendency to establish camps of what should be the way forward, as though one method of interactive story telling is somehow better than another.

I feel, though, that all are equally valid and that in the future we will see people choosing a game based upon how it tells a story as much as what the gameplay delivers.

Researching the Unexpected

The key to establishing authentic detail is plenty of research – geography, terminology, clothing, equipment or historical facts, for instance. The level of authenticity can determine how deeply players will immerse themselves into the world that's been created.

In the early stages of Revolution Software's game, Broken Sword – The Sleeping Dragon, I was looking for some historical hook that would give a good starting point to build the story around. I knew that we wanted to tie the game back to the first Broken Sword game, and in a way that would complete the trilogy in a tidy manner. With this in mind I started exploring connections to John Dee, who was mentioned in the earlier games. It wasn't long before I turned up a reference to something called the Voynich Manuscript.

This was exactly the starting point I needed – a genuine historical document written in a bizarre code that, to this day, no one has been able to decipher. This meant that the contents of the manuscript could be invented to match the needs of the story – the perfect device upon which to hang a historical mystery. Tying in a Templar power conspiracy was relatively straightforward, but what was it that the Voynich Manuscript hid within its code? We decided that it held the secret to unlocking the power of the Earth itself.

Coincidences can be more than a little spooky. When I started reading up on ley lines – because the idea is that the Earth's energy travels along these channels – my research kept pointing to many of the same things over and again. Not only did many of the ley line references lead to Glastonbury – which we used in the game – but there were also a number of them that mentioned York, where Revolution Software is based.

I read a little further and found that a number of the churches inside the old walls of the city were built along a straight ley line, including the huge York Minster. Ever curious, a couple of us went up to the top of the Minster tower and looked out over the city, expecting at best to see a vague approximation to a line. But there, in a perfectly straight line as clear as day, were the towers and spires of half a dozen churches as well as Clifford's Tower, all lining up with the junction of the two rivers, Ouse and Foss.

The coincidences continued. The land at the river junction is actually named St George's Field and the hero of the games is also named George. Even spookier is the fact that this land used to belong to the Templars. When we came down from the tower we were to get an even bigger surprise.

Outside the Minster a statue has been erected of the Roman Emperor, Constantine, a man who brought Christianity to the Roman Empire. The statue has him seated and looking at the pommel of his sword in a contemplative way. Yet the sculptor created the statue with the blade of the sword broken!

Although the York material didn't make it into the game, this research helped establish a feel and flavour that ensured the game as a whole really did have an air of authenticity. When you've made striking connections through research on the internet and actually seen genuine ley lines for yourself, you get to thinking that there's a kernel of truth in the stories you're making up and the whole becomes so much more believable.

Going with the flow

Ensuring that a game works as a whole is very important to the satisfaction the player will feel as they complete it. As with story and research, the flow of a game can make or break the experience.

I'm not, of course, talking about the story flow – although in some games this may well be tied very closely to what I'm covering here. What I mean is the logic flow of the game. Are there any dead ends, which cause the player to restore an earlier save game in order to progress? Do the conversations with these two separate characters still make sense if they are triggered in a different order?

Some games have a simple logic flow, which link sections of the game in a way that relies on finishing one section before completing another. There's no going back and no complex sets of variables that have to be taken into account, other than those connected with the player character's health, weapons or abilities. On the whole, these games are relatively straightforward when it comes to both designing the logic flow and testing its soundness.

Games that rely on the player visiting each section a number of times have the greatest chance for the logic flow to go wrong. Performing tasks or actions in one section that has an effect in another will always be at the whim of a complex set of variables that must be carried throughout the game. Development of the logic flow can be both time-consuming and potentially expensive, if it isn't done right. The less rigorously it's planned out, the more chance there is that the testing and fixing period will highlight serious problems that will lead to the game being delivered late.

Flow charts and diagrams are an important part of the development of the main gameplay and logic threads, along with detailed documentation at every level. Probably more important, however, is the ability to hold the image of the logic flow in your head and think it through on an almost daily basis, checking and re-checking that it is completely sound. In order to develop the logic flow successfully, the designer (lead designer, director, whatever) should live with this structure as though it's a second circulatory system flowing through his/her very being.

The downside to this is that you tend to wake in the middle of the night with concerns about how you're going to get the hero from the mountain village to the heart of New York without it feeling too contrived. And when you drift away from the conversation – eyes glazing over – in the middle of a dinner with friends, you'd better hope that they're incredibly good friends. Not everyone will understand the way that the design of a game takes over your life.

Sometimes, even with the best planning in the world and thorough testing, logic bugs can slip through. You've played it through time and time again yourself. So have the rest of the team and the publisher's test department. Yet, the first person who buys the game on release will happen to find the one logic bug that everyone missed.

And that's when, as you berate yourself for missing the problem, you really get the sleepless nights...

Giving the customer what they want

The old saying, "The customer is always right", is often taken too literally and many customers believe it allows them rights and privileges beyond what should reasonably be expected. However, the one thing that we must remember is that the customer is always right to choose only that which meets their requirements. A freelance provider of services to the games industry, when dealing with customers, must be very aware of that, because the moment they feel that this is not the case is the moment when they would no longer require those services.

Regardless of how a person may feel about the work they've taken on, once they have agreed to undertake it they must treat it with a fully professional attitude and deliver what has been defined. The temptation to adjust or deviate from the requirements of the customer must be resisted at all costs. Even if it's felt that those changes would improve the product being contributing to.

It may well be that part of the remit is to do exactly that. To work up new ideas and suggest areas where improvements could be made. They have decided that this particular expertise and experience is what their project needs to inject freshness into the process. But even then, finding out where the boundaries lie is an important thing to do. Without knowing these boundaries, not only will there be a risk of alienating the customer by re-working areas that they may well be perfectly happy with, but time will have been wasted if the work is rejected. If it falls outside the boundaries of the person's role in the project, then it will also be work that they will not be able to charge for.

Because finding out what the customer wants is of prime importance, only by asking plenty of questions will the knowledge be gained to deliver what the customer wants. Assumptions should never be made that are based upon initial perceptions of the project, because the likelihood is that it will be nothing like those assumptions. A clear definition of the project would be an ideal place to start, along with a clear statement of the required role. If the role overlaps with those of other people, it would be wise to ask if those people could be included in any briefing sessions so that all parties are working as a team.

Sometimes the role that the client has in mind isn't clearly defined because they are unsure what they need. By asking questions, it not only helps define the service provider's role, but could also help the customer define their own place in the working relationship.

Once the answers have been obtained and the work defined, it's always worth summarising this in a document, which should consist of a brief breakdown of the work involved. Estimates of all times should be done as accurately as possible, particularly if it's the early stages of the project and the work involved may have a big impact on the schedule. Then, when the work is delivered, it should not be late. It's vitally important that each agreed milestone is met.

If you don't deliver what the customer wants, then the customer is always right to not be interested in working with you again.

Fun, fun, fun!

> Danny: Don't worry yourself. I'll find the proof we need.
>
> Estelle: You?! You couldn't find the floor unless it was covered in beer.

The above comes from a document of ideas I'm developing for a game project. For me it illustrates what games should be about – the player having fun while they are working their way through the gameplay.

This week's column was actually going to be about something else entirely, but I felt that I was in danger of taking myself too seriously (particularly after the sombre nature of the last column) and decided it was time to lighten up and have some fun. After all, that's what games are meant to be about. Aren't they?

Sometimes it seems, when reading the gaming news sites, that games are increasingly serious in nature, so it was a breath of fresh air when I was given the chance of script-editing the English version of an excellent comedy game. Not only was it good to work on this title, it also re-kindled my interest in designing comedy games, so this week I've been putting some time into two different comedy game projects of my own and it's been great fun to do so.

Comedy is something that's subjective at the best of times, so what works for one person may very well fall flat for another. But as long as it falls flat on its face in a muddy puddle, all may not be lost. What I mean by this is that for a broad appeal, the comedy may need to work on more than one level.

I'm a firm believer that there's a long way to go with comedy in games and it's certainly an area I want to explore over the next few years. This ranges from cartoon–style to sitcom–style to more subtle, film style comedy. It also ranges from comedy aimed at children to comedy aimed at adults, with a centre ground that appeals to both.

Where, for instance, is the game equivalent of Toy Story or Finding Nemo? I'm not talking about the games that use the license in a superficial way, but ones that use the characters as they were used in the film, to create moments of genuine humour through the way the characters interact with one another. And if it is the player who triggers the humour through the gameplay interaction, then they are part of the unfolding comedy and it becomes a much more rewarding experience.

When I was developing part of the game, In Cold Blood, I decided to put in a couple of characters sitting near to each other. When the player character talks with them he discovers that they are having a tiff and not on speaking terms – she's jealous because he lent his scarf to a female officer. They start talking to one another through the player character, and the humour of the situation unfolds by the player talking to each one in turn, "Can you tell him that I'm not speaking to him until he apologises…"

This situation had nothing to do with the main plot of the game, but was an excellent way of adding richness by giving the feeling that there was more going on than just the story related scenes and by having some fun in the process.

Just imagine, though, if the main plot of a game unfolded through a regular series of such humorous scenes, how much more fun that could be.

Secret Panels

I was reading a weblog posting that made the claim of scripting weaknesses in some aspects of Doom 3. It struck me that, from the description, the underlying problem wasn't the scripting but the design behind it. A person can only script what's been designed, after all.

The issue the weblog picked up on centres on secret panels. The ones that open after the player has passed them by, revealing – usually by shooting you in the back – that monsters have suddenly appeared in the corridor behind you.

Now I've always had this problem with secret panels in general because, even in the most fantastical of settings, I can rarely see the justification for their existence. The more realistic the setting, the more any justification struggles to gain ground.

Okay, in a fantasy setting, when the players get to the heart of the castle they may find a secret panel behind the king's throne that hides something very precious, but you wouldn't expect to find such panels spread all through the castle. Would you?

What I want to know is, did the panels exist before the world/castle/high-tech base was populated with monsters? If so, what was the reason for their existence? Could a person never trust their colleagues and so must use them to store belongings? What's wrong with good old-fashioned locks?

Perhaps I'm looking for my answers in the wrong place and the base has been subject to the whims of a television home-improvement, makeover programme:

"You know what would go really well in here? A secret panel. I know what you're thinking, that they're a little passé, but just imagine the tricks you can play on your colleagues on a Monday morning. You dress up in the rubber costume from the fancy-dress shop and hide behind the secret panel waiting for them to arrive…"

But what really gets me smiling to myself is the thought of putting the monsters behind the secret panels. Presumably there was someone with a big evil plan that felt it was a good idea, making sure there was no food or water so they'd be good and angry when you triggered their appearance:

"Just hide in there, will you please?"

"Do I have to?"

"Yes you do. I'm the arch villain, sorry, antagonist – it says in my contract, you know – so you have to do what I tell you."

"It's always me. Why not one of the others?"

"The others don't have your flair for terrifying the crap out of unsuspecting, gun-toting, space marines."

"I bet you say that to all the monsters."

"Only the ugly ones."

"Oh, you…"

"Come on, I haven't got all day, you know."

"But I'm claustrophobic and this is such a small space…"

"For heaven's sake, you're a goddamn monster!"

"Oooh! So now you're saying that we don't have normal rights and feelings?"

"That's all I need, a sulking monster. GET BEHIND THE PANEL!"

"RRAAAWRR!"

"Okay, I may have been a little harsh, there. Now, will you please take my head out of your mouth…?"

Showing Character

Deciding the type of characterisation for the main character of a game can be one of the most important parts of concept development. If the character doesn't suit the needs of the game, there is a good chance that the game as a whole will suffer as a direct result.

If the game's story is one of its most important aspects, coming up with an idea for a main character may follow the initial outline of the story. Once the character starts to form, this feeds back into the story and the two play off each other, becoming more and more complex as other characters, particularly the antagonist, are introduced. The result of this should mean that the story and character are completely at one with each other and, if the design process has been completely successful, with the gameplay, too.

An alternative method is to create the character first and then decide the story he will be involved with, which can be a much more difficult route. Of course, no character can be created completely in a vacuum, so the design team will likely have a good idea of the type of story the character will be involved in before the character is developed.

In many character-driven stories, the main character goes through a transformation of sorts as the story unfolds and is no longer the same person at the end as he was when the story began. This transformation may not always be desirable, particularly if the character is expected to become central to a whole series of games. For a continuing series, character progression in each story should be relatively minimal or the changes could take him/her away from what made the character right for the central role in the first place. One of the reasons the James Bond films have been so successful over the years is that as a character he's been pretty well defined and he tends to end the film the same person that started it. The stories revolve around his job rather than him as a person and are what is known as event-driven rather than character-driven. Many games fall into this category and so the Bond level of characterisation is about right for these, offering up many chances for sequels.

You will often read in books that you should avoid stereotypes at all cost, but sometimes the main character needs to be nothing more than a stereotype because this may help the player get a handle on what the character represents from the very beginning of the game. The gameplay may be all-important and any story and characterisation is superficial at best. The requirements from the character are not what he/she is like as a person, but what their gameplay abilities are – how high can they jump, how fast can they run, and so forth. If Mario suddenly started questioning his place in the world and became angst-ridden, then players would rightly complain that he's no longer the character they came to love. Mario has become his own stereotype, but one that works perfectly within the context of the games he's used in.

Naming your characters can be much more difficult than creating them in the first place. If James Bond had been called Reginald Periwinkle, Ian Fleming may never have sold his first Bond novel. Sometimes I feel that every name I ever choose for a character could be better (with the exception of Scout the One-Eyed Cat, of course). I always know when a name definitely won't work, but finding one that definitely will work can be so elusive.

Although getting a good name is important, it's also got to fit the style of character. A strong and bold name wouldn't necessarily fit a character who's really just an ordinary guy thrust into a series of events outside of his control. Yes, he may rise to the challenge and become a hero, but choosing a name that fits his initial nature can emphasise just how far he's come in his journey through the story.

Dialogue? What dialogue? Part One

Not a simple subject even at the best of times, I realised as I was writing this that what I wanted to touch on could only be done by spreading it over two columns.

I've worked almost exclusively on games where the dialogue between characters is developed to a high degree to maximise the relevance to the game, staying true to the characters and laced with high interest and humour. This often affects the way that I respond to dialogue in other games. While there are many games that handle dialogue very well, others contain character speeches that really don't fit the true meaning of the word dialogue.

Many game developers choose not to have the main character speak for numerous valid reasons. For instance, the player may create their own character from a choice of templates and having the character speak would mean having to record a huge number of line variations to make the dialogue fit the character. The downside to this non-speaking player character is that, because conversations with other characters are often one-sided, it can give the impression that the player is simply listening to a series of mini monologues.

Sometimes these monologues are triggered by proximity of the player character, which can in itself create an artificial feeling because suddenly, this character you've never met before, is giving you plot-relevant information without being asked. Even in games where conversations are triggered and controlled by the player, because the player character doesn't speak, the other character's lines are often structured in a way that gives more information than you'd normally expect. In a film or a novel, the main character would only get the information they need by a dynamic exchange of dialogue. When characters are not reacting to anything the other character is saying, the speech always comes across as a little surreal and this in turn strains at the immersion the player gets from playing the game.

It may well be that monologue conversations are a necessary part of certain types of games, though I find that hard to imagine. If this were the case, however, writing monologues would need to look towards doing so in a way that will give the maximum dramatic effect and may lead to an expansion of existing writing vocabulary. Not an insignificant task.

The main burden of the monologue approach is that the character speaking is effectively doing the work of two characters by second-guessing what the player character wants and providing detailed answers. This actually has a knock-on effect of weakening the main character because they simply listen to the monologues in a very passive way. What's the point of developing a dynamic character that fights for his life while trying to save the world, if he shows no reaction to important revelations from the other characters?

When games are becoming increasingly realistic in their rendering of characters, adversaries and locations, it often feels that elements of the game that don't match this approach are things that can destroy the suspension of disbelief and prevent the player from achieving a fully immersive experience.

Because two-way conversations – dialogue   are such an important part of our everyday lives, monologues will always come across as artificial because they do not represent the way we talk. As games continue to become increasingly sophisticated the artificial feel will only increase.

Dialogue? What dialogue? Part Two

There are many games where dialogue is an important part of the gameplay experience, yet it's often handled in a way that strikes me as being far too convenient. Supporting characters almost fall over themselves in their eagerness to give the player the information he needs to progress. The following lines illustrate a simplified version of a common structure.

"Hello, we've never met before."

"That's okay. If you get me Madonna's autograph I'll tell you the secret password."

What just happened, here? As a player I was given game information too suddenly and I was taken aback – I feel cheated that it happened too easily. How on earth did this character know I wanted the secret password? Was I aware that I wanted this information?

There are two problems that arise from an exchange as short as that – the structure of the conversation itself and the imparting of game information.

We all know how conversations work from experience, even if we cannot write. This knowledge comes from interacting with other people on a day to day basis, over-hearing conversations on the bus, and from the wealth of TV and film we're all exposed to, as well as many other examples. When we experience a conversation that falls outside of what we expect, it immediately puts a strain on our suspension of disbelief. The following lines approach the interaction in a more convincing way.

"Hi, I'm Brad Green."

"So?"

"I understand you know the password to the Kitty Klub."

"You understand wrong."

"Tommy Smith told me -"

"Tommy Smith talks out of his backside. Now get lost."

Admittedly, the player didn't find out about the autograph, but we believe the structure because it fits with our experiences. We have also created dramatic conflict because the player character (and the player) has not achieved what he expected to. This failure to get the information suddenly throws up the need for more gameplay in order that the player character can finally convince this person to give him the password. Or to find out why Tommy Smith was lying. Or something else entirely. The actual gameplay and the route to the information will take different forms depending on the genre of the game involved.

Dialogue must not only serve the needs of drama and gameplay, it must also be written in a way that's in keeping with the nature of the characters involved. What if the holder of the password was incredibly chatty, but only ever talked about himself? The conflict could be made humorous rather than sinister. What if they were sad, or drunk, or in fear for their life? What if they were in the pay of someone who wants you to have the information, but they've got to make it seem like you're forcing it out of them? The potential for variety is endless.

The key to building good dialogue structure is to start by understanding what the agendas of the characters are so that you have two points of view when writing each scene. It might be something simple like the other character not wanting to talk with anyone. If it's one of the major characters in the story, though, it's likely that the agenda the character has will relate to the plot and may well change depending on how far along the plot the player has progressed.

Even with the best structure in the world, dialogue can often fail if it's written in a way that sounds clumsy when spoken aloud. The only solution here is to speak the lines out loud, act them out, and any weaknesses will quickly be evident.

Of course, that introduces a different type of problem. When you're in the middle of a gritty dramatic conversation with yourself and your partner walks into the room, having her fall about laughing makes you wish you'd rented office space away from home.

Dialogue? What dialogue? Part Three

That this subject had stretched itself to a third column shows the importance I feel that dialogue plays in story and character driven games. As I touched on briefly last time, if vital game information is revealed through dialogue, conversations should not be separated out from the overall gameplay. This means that because dialogue becomes an important part of the gameplay, the player should therefore have at least a modicum of control during conversations.

The player can become frustrated when it seems they are simply a passenger during long periods of exposition. However, if the player gets the opportunity to work for that exposition, the rewarding nature of the interaction increases the empathy with the player character and the involvement in the developing story.

To obtain the best possible fit, dialogue must become part of the overall game design process or the aims of the dialogue and the gameplay may be at odds with each other. In other words, a structure should be developed for the way that the dialogue scenes are triggered so that it matches the structure of the other aspects of developing gameplay.

This isn't to say that actual lines of dialogue need to be written as part of the design process, simply that the scenes should be identified and what information is going to be discussed and passed on.

In many respects, it's much better not to write any dialogue at first as it can have an effect on the speed of implementation and testing. Having just the bare bones of the scenes with variables being set, means exactly the same thing to the progress of the game, providing that the people implementing the game have a clear idea of what is happening in each scene. The dialogue can be written and added in at a later point and may benefit from the writer being able to see the game in progress and match the feel of the dialogue to what's on screen.

Something that always strikes me as poor dialogue structure, when I see it in a game, is when avenues of dialogue repeat unnecessarily. Unless the dialogue structure is specifically designed so that the discussion of a subject can expand in detail – introducing new lines for example – the chance to talk about that subject again should not be available. When a scene, or part of a scene, repeats word for word, I feel it undermines the hard work that the writer has put in, reducing any drama and spoiling the professional appearance.

Some scenes, if not all, are best developed with the writer and designer working together. Scenes aren't just about giving the player important game information, but also for developing the characters, working through sub-plots and for creating dramatic tension and conflict. Subtext, while not something that's been particularly strong in games so far, will come increasingly into play, as character acting and facial expressions continue to improve and tools are developed that allow subtle acting to become a common part of games.

Only when a designer and writer both understand the story, character and gameplay needs of all scenes will they be able to deliver something very special.

Motivation and Conflict

Like many other aspects of game development, motivation is two-pronged. Not only do you need to consider the motivation of what drives the player character through the game's story, you also need to consider how to keep the player motivated to continue playing the game.

All games, whether they have a story or not, should ensure that the player is sufficiently motivated to continue playing on a moment-to-moment basis. This is part of the fundamentals of good gameplay and is not what I want to discuss this time around. I want to concentrate on the player character's motivation and the conflicts that stand in the way. For only with conflict can we get something that approaches true drama.

Motivation comes from a combination of things; the personality of the character, his connection to what's at stake and his ability to discern a clear direction that will take him towards his goals. If he doesn't care enough or believe that he can do what needs to be done, then his motivation to even try is going to be severely lacking.

The developing story drives the motivation of the player character. If the broad gameplay goals tie in with the story goals, then the blending of the two will provide additional impetus to the player. If there is a strong story reason to go to the abandoned school, and not just because it's a cool location, then you believe the character's motivation for going there much more.

Because there are other characters in the game, you also need to take into account their motivation, particularly the antagonist. Without good motivation, the player will begin to question why the bad guy is doing what he's doing. It also needs to be made clear that the antagonist is getting on with his plans off screen or it will feel like he's just sitting around waiting for the player to turn up at the end of the next level.

Drama is created when the expectations of two characters, driven by their individual motivation, comes into conflict. This could be something as simple as one character trying to get through a doorway and another character preventing them. More often than not, the conflict will be more complicated or less clearly definable. Sometimes conflict can be a mixture of three or more characters and it may not always be clear who is conflicting with who – sides may shift and change through the course of an exchange that in turn leads to more conflict.

Conflict may appear to be an odd way of providing motivation for the characters, but if they were the type of characters that backed away from conflict and adversity, would they be the type of characters you'd want in a game? Certainly, the player character should be sufficiently motivated that he will continue, even when faced with personal danger, the threat of global annihilation, and sarcastic ridicule.

If the player character is taking a path that brings him into conflict with the plans of the antagonist, then he's clearly on the right lines. If that isn't enough motivation in itself, then we'll throw in some poisonous spiders and snakes for good measure.

Gameplay Mechanics Part One

About eight years ago, I was sent a game design handwritten on two sheets of A4 paper with one very small map drawn in pencil. Most of the writing described a story, rather than gameplay, but it was clear that the guy who sent it thought that we'd just take it and implement a game from this. I think it's fair to say that nowadays the general gaming public have a bit more idea of what goes into making a game than they did those few short years ago, though it's always useful to look into why we do the things we do.

One of the hardest parts about game design is turning all the cool ideas into realistic and consistent game mechanics and documenting them in such a way that the coding and implementation will happen without any misunderstandings. This isn't about designing cool levels; this is about developing the basic building blocks with which to design those levels.

Very often, the basic premise for a game is there from the very beginning. The team knows that they want to create an FPS/RPG/RTS/Platformer/Adventure/etc. and they have to build from there. What gameplay mechanics are they going to create that gives their game an edge in today's marketplace? Clearly a team-wide brainstorming session is called for, where anyone can throw ideas onto the table.

A good brainstorming session should give the team more ideas than they could ever hope to incorporate into a single game. It should never be about analysing those ideas – that comes later – but should be a way of getting everything recorded. If it's run with the principle of there being no stupid ideas, it will encourage everyone to think outside of the box. Sometimes the "stupid" ideas are the best ones for making everyone feel at ease and may even inspire great ideas in a tangential way.

For the purpose of this column, I'm going to work through an idea that I've just brainstormed with myself (don't worry, it's perfectly safe if I wash my hands afterwards). Thinking about a way to add something into the mix, I came up with the idea of Rocket Boots. In a normal brainstorming session there would be a few humorous comments, no doubt, so just imagine that someone somewhere has made a witty remark about Elton John's "Rocket Man". However, along with everything else generated from the session, it goes down on the list of possible ideas.

The thing about ideas is that they so often need to mature and develop, becoming full-bodied as they work away in the subconscious of the individual team members' minds. The list of ideas should be written up and distributed, immediately following the brainstorming session, but the design meeting to develop those ideas should be left for at least a couple of days. If possible, so that everyone has had the time to think about them, allow a week to pass by before calling the meeting.

Therefore, with that in mind, if you all have a think about Rocket Boots over the next week, when I resume this topic next time I'll look at how the idea could be developed into a possible gameplay mechanic.

Gameplay Mechanics Part Two

So, it's a week later and we've called the design team together to discuss the results of the brainstorming session. We've all typed up our thoughts or scribbled notes in the margins of the brainstorming list. The project is in the early stages, so we're all really excited about it. We don't care if it's going to be a long session because we're going to have some fun.

Of course, design is a serious business and should always be approached with a professional manner, but if the development of ideas isn't interlaced with a liberal dose of fun, how will the fun get through to the final game?

Working through a number of ideas, with varying degrees of success, we get to the one that I proposed, the rocket boots. A couple of people express concern that it may be a bit of a cliché, so I suggest that we have a mini-brainstorm and think about possible ways of developing the idea further. If we don't think it is going anywhere after ten minutes we should put it to one side and move on.

We start with possible variations on the rocket boot idea and we get a few suggestions: jet boots, spring boots and anti-gravity boots. That last idea we think might have legs (ho, ho) so we concentrate on this for a time.

Worried that having the anti-gravity boots on all the time may prove to be a gameplay problem, we look at how we could limit their functionality and make that limit become part of the gameplay.

Because many gameplay mechanics are developments of old ideas or simply because players expect sophistication, it's always better to refine the ideas into something more than the bare essentials.

With this in mind, someone suggests that the boots should be anti-gravity pulse boots. A short burst of anti-gravity would shoot the player character into the air, but they would then be subject to the pull of gravity. It would be down to the player to work out how to use that sudden, huge leap to their advantage. This is a good development, but there is now a concern that the player will simply keep jumping their character continually.

The next suggestion involves a modification so that the boots take thirty seconds to recharge and the battery packs for them only have ten charges. Finding the battery packs for the boots becomes an additional layer of gameplay. Of course, at this stage, any numbers discussed are simply pulled out of the air and will require full game testing and tweaking before a proper gameplay balance is found.

The design session would normally continue looking at the other brainstorming ideas, but for the moment, let's concentrate on the anti-gravity pulse boots. Although the mechanic is a feasible one, we need to be sure that it fits with the overall concept of the game. If it's a Victorian mystery adventure, then the idea of the boots would never have been developed in the first place, so the fact that we entertained the idea to the degree we did implies that the basic concept fits with the game premise.

The next stage in the development of any mechanic is to assess the impact it will have on the overall gameplay, the level designs and building and the other mechanics like shooting weapons. Then there are the specific details that have to be considered – the application of physics during flight, the damage to the player for missing the overhead walkway, etc. While looking at these aspects, the design team must be its own devil's advocate, because if any issues are not discovered and ironed out at this stage, then they are bound to surface later when they will be much more costly to remedy.

Once the details of the mechanic have been worked through to everyone's satisfaction, the task of documenting it must be undertaken. Never underestimate the value of documentation. Without clearly written documents you have no record of the details of the mechanic. Artists will be unclear what they have to do. Programmers may take months before they are able to work on this mechanic and you're bound to have forgotten some detail in the interim, so get it down while the idea is still fresh still excites you.

After going through this process, you may think you've done well by completely designing a cool mechanic. Fine – pat yourself on the back. But make sure you have plenty of energy for the other 99% of the game that still has to be designed...

Level 17 Made Me Cry

This may seem like I'm being a little slow on the uptake, but I wanted to finish off my two-part piece on mechanics design before writing this. Besides, it's always best to ruminate on these things for a little while before launching into commentary. Reacting too swiftly to news, people's statements and press releases can give results that are coloured by an initial emotional reaction instead of reasoned thought.

Some of the things I've read about Spielberg's and Zemeckis's recent comments fall into the category of knee-jerk defensive reaction. To summarise, they both feel that while games are developing their story telling well, there is still some way to go before they will be on a par with films. I must say that I agree with this view and it's difficult to see why anyone would disagree. There are some fabulous things being done in games and we should be proud of how far the industry has developed in a relatively short time, but at the same time, we need to be realistic about where we are in the larger scheme of things.

Having a go at Spielberg seems a little misguided to me. Here is a man with vision, who has created a large number of excellent, successful films; yet people have jumped on his comments as if he doesn't know what he's talking about. While he may not know everything about the games industry, we should be listening to what this man says from the viewpoint of someone on the outside looking in. We should consider how we might use his experience and vision to move game development forward.

Specific attention has been aimed at Spielberg's quote, "I think the real indicator will be when somebody confesses that they cried at level 17." Many seem to think that it's an indication that he's out of touch with games because no one refers to levels in games any more. Come on, just because we may refer to them as chapters or missions, to all intents and purposes they are still levels, particularly in the way that many games implement them.

To ridicule Spielberg's statement only shows how little is known about the larger issues; about how story works on many levels. Most reactions I've read use the same example to refute his claim – the death of Aeris in Final Fantasy VII. If we have only the one example to turn to, it actually shows how right Spielberg is, particularly when you take into account that it's the death of a main character – an extreme plot development in any situation. What about crying because the main character's just been told he has cancer? Or with relief that her kidnapped son is alive and well? Or with joy because the boy meets girl subplot has resulted in a meaningful relationship? This is the real significance behind Spielberg's statement.

From the perspective of people looking from outside the industry, games have clearly yet to move us in the way that films do. One highly emotional scene from a single game that has forty hours of gameplay doesn't even come close and shows how far we have yet to go.

Because Spielberg has said something that make games look inferior to movies, some people have simply become defensive. Instead, we should be using this as a springboard to making games reach the heights and tell the stories that not only equal those told in films, but also surpass them. There is an amazing wealth of talent in the industry that can help achieve this, but the key is being realistic about where we are now.

Shall we interface?

Have you ever picked up your joypad or approached your keyboard and found that you struggled to play the game that's in the machine because the interface felt wrong? Have you ever given up on a game simply because you were fighting the interface more than playing the game? When the interface creates these feelings in the player, it acts as a barrier to enjoyment of the game, instead of a means by which players can immerse themselves into the game world with ease.

The development of a set of interface mechanics can be a major concern. If you don't get it right, the whole perception of the playability of your game will be judged by how the interface affects the player's enjoyment. It's likely that most projects go through a period where the interface doesn't feel right or needs improvement – the trick is to discover the problems before the game is released.

It is at this point that some of you may be wondering about the interface problems in Broken Sword – The Sleeping Dragon. For many people, the keyboard interface on this game was a major barrier to their enjoyment and is actually a powerful lesson in the dangers of taking things for granted.

Revolution Software was clear from the outset that the game should move away from the point-and-click interface that was the trademark of the adventure. Many reviews of other adventures or articles about the adventure genre often talked about the point-and-click interface in a derogatory manner. It was felt that such a PC-specific interface was holding the genre back from moving to a wider range of gaming platforms. With this in mind, the development of The Sleeping Dragon was geared towards a lead on the PS2 and Xbox consoles with an interface that matched the joypads that the two machines used.

The joypad-based interfaces worked very well and suited perfectly the aims of broadening the genre. However, this success blinded us to the problem of the PC interface and here was where we took for granted that on the keyboard it would just work. Moving the player character around the game environments in a screen-relative control mode simply isn't as easy on a keyboard as it is with a joypad.

Perhaps it's the nature of the keys themselves; perhaps it's something about the difference between using fingers instead of thumbs. Whatever the reason behind the difficulty, it should have been seen earlier so that something could have been done about it. Giving an additional option to switch to character-relative control may have been all that was needed, but it was something we missed and it's certainly a lesson I have learned. Unfortunately, a lesson learned the hard way.

Of course, it could be that the worry over the point-and-click interface led to a slight over-reaction, particularly when you consider that other games use this type of interface. PC based RPGs regularly use a point-and-click interface with no worry about whether it's outmoded. Even Doom 3 uses a variation for when the player wishes to interact with objects he comes across in the game world.

When looking at the interface for your game, be aware of what other games are doing and learn from approaches that work well. You can also learn from interfaces that make mistakes, by ensuring that you don't make those same mistakes.

The interface should be the player's means of connecting with a great game, not a barrier to having fun.

Puzzling Through the Obstacles

One of the criticisms levelled at Adventure Games these days is that they can feel a little old fashioned. I'm increasingly of the opinion that this is because they contain these things we refer to as "puzzles". This term can then create the wrong idea in people's heads as to what sort of game adventures are. Of course, there are adventures that probably fit this perception very well, but more and more adventures are developing a kind of gameplay that makes it difficult to think of the player as solving puzzles.

The word puzzle, to me, suggests gameplay that involves pulling levers in the right combination or fiddling around with sliders. While there isn't necessarily anything wrong with this type of gameplay, it does have a "static" kind of feel to it, particularly at a time when the majority of gamers want dynamic games. Some of the other aspects of adventure games – collecting clues, using inventory objects, developing story and so forth – are already being included in other genres, so it seems that adventures could find a broader player base if they concentrated on just these aspects. And stopped using the word, puzzle.

I believe that a much better term is "obstacle". This has a much wider relevance and can be applied to almost any genre of game. For my purposes, an obstacle is anything that the player must overcome in order to progress in the game. A puzzle may be an obstacle, but obstacles aren't restricted to puzzles. An obstacle is also the end of level boss in a platform game, or winning the gold trophy in a race game in order to unlock the special car.

One of the beauties of thinking in terms of obstacles is that you can take a much wider approach to your thinking than when concentrating on puzzles. In many respects, the antagonist, working his way through the plot of the game in opposition to the hero, is a large obstacle that lasts the length and breadth of the game and the other obstacles simply feed into that. At least they can if they are designed with an eye on how they fit with the overall story, design and the style of gameplay.

Obstacles can overlap and interweave with one another, in the same way that subplots do in a good film or novel. It could be that the player has a number of different obstacles to overcome at any one time and that they could be overcome in any order. Alternatively, in order to overcome one obstacle, another has to be beat to get the device, clue or information needed to address the first.

Sometimes an obstacle needs a multiple-stage approach to beating it, with some of those stages opening up new obstacles. Suppose, for instance, your character needs to get into the courtyard, but there's a wall blocking the way. The character can't just climb over, as it's too high, so he brings across the nearby dustbin to stand on. Only then, he finds that broken glass has been cemented into the top of the wall and he'll cut himself to ribbons if he tries to climb over. Therefore, he needs to find something like a heavy rug to drape over the wall. The only one he can find nearby is being used by a tramp who won't give it to him unless he gets a bottle of whiskey in return...

Of course, if it were a GTA type of game, the player would simply blow the tramp away and take the rug. However, if you had the anti-gravity pulse boots I talked about a few weeks ago, the wall would only be a minor obstacle, as the player character would simply jump over the wall without worrying.

What the above shows is that while obstacles can be built upon to provide increasing gameplay, the same obstacles in different styles of game will require different solutions and approaches by the player.

The trick is in making the obstacles challenging without giving the player the feeling that they are going nowhere.

Obstacles of Desire

One of my favourite obstacles in a game was in Beneath a Steel Sky. Though I worked on this game, I didn't contribute to the gameplay design; so I think it's okay for me to feel this way. One of the reasons I enjoyed my eleven years with Revolution was that I had such respect for the people I worked with.

The obstacle in question involved getting into a security building with the use of a grappling hook and cable. The route to getting these objects had a convoluted series of steps that involved finding a spanner, fitting the robot, Joey, with a welder shell, trading objects with others, distracting people, getting Joey to melt through a loose cable and then have him cut the anchor off a statue in order that you could use it as the hook. Mixed into this were other minor obstacles and much humour as you explored the world and put up with the sarcastic comments of a less than enthusiastic sidekick.

What worked best for me was the way that I never felt that I was simply solving a small puzzle and then moving onto the next one – the gameplay seemed more continuous and free flowing than that. Being able to wander around the world with relative freedom also helped give the impression that I was in control of what was going on.

Another obstacle I particularly admire is in Half-Life, where you must kill the monster with the test rocket engine. Of course, you must get past the monster a few times in order to get the fuel and power flowing to the engine and console, working out how to distract it temporarily as you work through the tasks involved. The elegance of the obstacle is that not only was it clear what your objective was, but it acted as a secondary obstacle to completing the other tasks. Then, when you completed the tasks and fired off the rocket engine, it was such a satisfying thing to do, rewarding you well for overcoming the obstacle.

One of the things that strikes me, is that a successful obstacle is one that doesn't give the impression that it's insurmountable, even if you're struggling to complete the tasks needed to beat it. If the objective is clear and the tools are to hand (though they may be difficult to obtain), then all that's left is for the player to put the parts together. Of course, simply put like that, it may seem as though making the obstacles easy is the key, but that's not the case. It's not about ease, but clarity – difficulty should arise from the way the route to beating the obstacle tests the skills of the player, not by making the steps along the route obscure or illogical.

There have been games in the past, where playing them has felt, at times, as if it's a battle with the designer. Searching for the important object was reduced to a mind-numbing pixel hunt, or leaping across the chasm could only be achieved by a professional gaming ninja with skills enough to press twenty buttons or keys at the same time.

When the designer of an obstacle begins to think, "There's no way the player will beat this one!" then it's time that the designer should be re-thinking his approach to obstacle design. Thankfully, few games have this flaw, today, but thinking carefully about obstacles will only improve the whole gaming experience for all of us.

Character Profiles

Part of my current job involves creating the character profiles for my client's project. Now, I can't go into the specific details of what I'm doing (for obvious reasons), but I thought I would reflect on how important it is to do this work. Although I've already discussed characters, in an earlier column, this edition deals with the profiles themselves.

Of course, you may think that if you're the only one working on your project, character profiles are not important – you know what your characters will do or how they'll behave in a given situation. However, while that may be true for a few main characters, it's unlikely to be the case for all of the characters you'll likely need in a story-based game. It's equally important to develop proper character profiles if you are a team of one, or part of a team of fifty.

Not only do character profiles act as a means of recording your thoughts on your main characters – how they behave and react – they also serve a fuller purpose of helping you work through the details of your supporting characters. The process of developing the profiles allows you flesh out the characters and make them much more rounded.

You may wonder why this is important for supporting characters, but if you want the character designer and modeller to transfer your ideas into polygon flesh, so to speak, then the more they have to go on the better the character will match the mental picture you had of each one. Likewise, if the animators have an understanding of what makes your characters tick, then they're much more likely to animate them in a rich and varied manner. As important as this side of things is, the real value of the profiles is how they can help you.

Months may pass from writing the story for your project and writing the scenes that take place between the characters. While you may remember the broad sweep with crystal clarity, it's likely that all of the subtlety you were thinking of at the time has been lost because you've spent the intervening time working on other aspects of the project, or even on another project altogether.

I'm not talking about the subtlety of the story, but of the characters. If Katie Eckersley has suffered from asthma since being six years old, how will that affect her outlook on life? Has she given into it and developed a hatred for all sports? Or has she seen it as a challenge and is now a champion swimmer? And how did that affect the relationship she had with her mother, who smothered her in attempting to protect Katie from harm?

Characters are so much more than one defining trait, though, and the profiles you develop should reflect this. Basic information like gender, age and build are always useful to include, simply because they start the ball rolling and get you into the other details more readily. What you include in your list will be down to your particular tastes and the needs of the game you're developing for, but it's better to have too much information than not enough. Some suggestions for included traits or information could be:

- The purpose of the character in the game.
- How they progress through the game.

- Speech oddities, accents and mannerisms.
- Occupation.
- Personal history or background.
- What they like to do in their spare time.
- Any special talents or abilities.
- Any handicaps or problems.
- How they dress.

This is a straightforward list, but it can be adapted or added to, particularly if your characters inhabit a fantastical universe, or it's important to build a highly subtle portrait of each character. However, there are things that it would be silly to include, like favourite colour – when was the last time you heard of the way two people interact with one-another being affected by their favourite colour?

One of the real beauties of working through your list of traits and information, filling out details for each character, is that it can be such fun. Not only do you get to make up small stories about each character's life and the type of person they are, it can give you new insights into the main story and how it can be subtly enriched by this wealth of detail you have just developed.

The characters come to life and the story and game become so much more immersive.

Back-Story

No, this isn't the story of how I'm in constant pain with my bad back. But now that I've brought it up, I wonder how much sympathy I can garner from mentioning the stabbing pains that run up and (That's enough, Ince. Get on with the column, you pathetic wimp – Ed.) Ahem.

Back-story falls into the same category as character profiles – you can write and design your game without it, but it will be so much richer if you've taken the time to develop it well.

The back-story should cover anything and everything that leads up to the events of the story covered in the game. Because the game world itself regularly contributes to the experience the player enjoys, details of how the game world came to be should be a major part of the detail.

You may have already chosen to include each character's personal back-story into the character profiles, but this shouldn't stop you looking at how the characters fit into the overall back-story. As already mentioned last week, the character profiles enable you and the team to get a handle on the characters themselves – what makes them tick. The back-story enables you to get a handle on the game as a whole, the story that unfolds and the world in which it all takes place.

Many elements of the back-story have a direct bearing on the game's story and gameplay. Sometimes this is revealed as important clues or information the player discovers as he progresses through the game; sometimes it's just background that adds to the flavour and richness, but has no direct influence on the story.

The development team should always know more about the world than they ever expect to put into the game. Some material may exist just to help the writer approach a particular scene in a way that makes it more believable.

One such instance is a scene in Broken Sword: The Sleeping Dragon. Petra is holding a gun on Nico and suggests that they have met previously, but doesn't enlighten Nico as to when that was. Here is a detail that, though created, was not fully revealed. Not only does it refer to a time and place outside of the current game world, it also adds a mystery as the player puzzles over this. If there are further sequels, more detail could be revealed, but for the follower of the series, thoughts about where it could have happened in the previous games (if at all) abound.

In a similar manner to working up character profiles, develop your back-story with a view to creating detail and answering questions about everything that has a possible bearing. What is the history of the weird race of cats? How did the zombies arrive on the strange moon? What is the story behind the gold artefact found at the bottom of a Scottish loch?

Unlike character profiles, it is not possible to break down the back-story into a series of headings to be filled in. Because the nature of your story is likely to be unique, the events that lead up to it will also be unique. Each game will have its own back-story, its own way of pulling everything together to make the story much more rewarding.

Don't be afraid to be quite open in your inventiveness – providing you maintain a consistency with your world. I don't have a bad back, but it would have made the story of the way I sit here and type these words so much more interesting if that were the case. The thought of a writer suffering for his art somehow seems more in keeping with a stereotype image.

However, I'll leave it for you to decide if that should belong in my character profile or my life's back-story.

Interaction Density

(A second piece on the subject.)

I came up with the term "Interaction Density" when I was part of a long forum discussion on the way there are no adventures targeted at 8-13 year old boys. Why did the likes of "Day of the Tentacle" and "Monkey Island" appeal to this age group when they came out, yet today's adventure games fail to do so?

Some of the answer lies in the fact that adventure games no longer have that element of fun about them that they once did. Where are the talking skulls, the spitting contests, the tentacles trying to take over the world? Where is the grandiose sense of adventure written big, with jokes and dialogue to match? Some people are of the opinion that the answer lies in recreating the style of the old games and everyone will be happy, but that fails to take into account the changing nature of the game market.

There is another aspect to the problem that has only come about in recent years since the CD became commonplace, the lack of high Interaction Density.

Back when games for the PC and the Amiga came on floppy discs, space was short, so every location was made to earn its keep. On each colourful screen existed a veritable plethora of fun characters to interact with, objects to pick up and hotspots to examine, along with the regular puzzle-solving gameplay. In other words, there was always lots for the player to do in each location – the high Interaction Density ensure that the player shouldn't become bored.

A thread over at the Adventure Games Forums caused me to think about why today's adventure games might not be attractive to 8–13 year olds (boys, mainly). Aside from the fact that very few of them have the pure fun element that older games like Monkey Island or Day of the Tentacle, most of today's adventures have a low Interaction Density.

Because older games had to make the most of limited floppy disc space, particularly on the Amiga, each location in an adventure was made to work hard for its keep. Each screen was filled with wonderful characters, objects to collect or interact with and hotspots to examine. Now, with the ability to cram ten times (or more) the number of locations onto a CD or DVD, even at very high resolution, the number of interactable items on each screen/location has reduced for the same amount of gameplay. The Interaction Density has decreased drastically, to the point in some places where there are strings of locations through which all the player character does is walk.

Game players of all ages don't simply want to wander around, particularly young kids with notoriously short attention spans, so when there is little to interact with, the natural conclusion to draw is that adventures are boring and not worth bothering with. Action games, in comparison, offer an almost constantly high Interaction Density and are always going to be a better draw to gamers who want to be always "doing stuff" in the games they play.

Clearly, the time has come to address this balance by thinking more creatively about the layout of adventures so that they offer the same level of Interaction Density they used to.

Part 3
Retirement

Steve Ince (of Broken Sword & More) Announces Retirement – His Thoughts...

(First published on Pixel Refresh.)

Games, Retirement and the Future

On June 20th 2023, I made an announcement that I am going to retire from working in the video games industry from February 2024.

For those who don't know (and there will be many), I have worked in the games industry for 30 years as a writer, artist and game designer. Some of my credits have included Beneath a Steel Sky, Broken Sword, So Blonde and The Witcher.

You can think about something for ages, worrying about whether it would be the right move as you look to your future, maybe giving you sleepless nights in the process. Such was the case for me as I thought about retiring from the video games industry. Yet as soon as I made my announcement I knew it was exactly the right thing.

It's not that I regret having worked in the industry for so long and am desperate to get out, simply that I am ready for new and different creative challenges, which at sixty-five I find rather exhilarating. I also want to concentrate more on my own projects –

writing and illustrating books, for instance – as I have so many exciting ideas I want to bring to life.

The games industry has been good to me, providing me with a career that has supported me over the last thirty years. Of course, none of that would have been possible without the start given to me by the wonderful people at Revolution Software. But that was only the beginning; during my time there I was also encouraged to push myself creatively and become more skilful with each passing year. And that's something I've strived to do ever since, giving my very best to all the projects I've been fortunate to work on.

There was, of course, life beyond Revolution as I turned freelance in 2004, though it scared me half to death at first. In fact, I didn't really find my feet for most of the first year. But thanks to initial clients who had faith in me and other writers that provided moral support, I was able to build my freelance business and soon began working for a regular stream of clients.

It has been enjoyable in different ways to work on all the projects I've been a part of, but there are some that will always hold a special place in my heart and mind. *Beneath a Steel Sky* for being the first game I worked on; *Broken Sword* for the groundbreaking game it was at the time; and *In Cold Blood* for being the game I first did any writing on. *So Blonde*, too, for being the first full game I wrote and designed after turning freelance.

One of the things I've loved the most over the years has been creating, developing and writing great characters, particularly when I get the chance to do so from scratch. So games like *Special Enquiry Detail* and *Rhianna Ford and the Da Vinci Letter* are also important for this aspect alone. Characters are vitally important to the way I approach my stories.

Turning freelance also threw up other opportunities, such as writing articles for online websites, which then led to the publisher A&C Black (later bought by Bloomsbury) asking me to write a book, *Writing for Video Games*. At the time of doing so, they and I were happy with the finished manuscript, but with hindsight and further experience under my belt I think it could have had a different emphasis. However, I know of at least one person who got into games writing after being inspired by the book, so perhaps I shouldn't be so self-critical.

I'd always wanted to write books from being a teenager (though mainly a desire for science fiction) and taught myself to type on a small, manual typewriter my parents bought for me. (On a side note, it's amazing how my spelling improved through not wanting to make mistakes that I'd have to correct with Tip-Ex.) So it was only natural I'd turn to writing fiction in the spare time I had between game writing and drawing online comic strips.

Juggling so many things meant that progress was slow and although I eventually amassed a substantial collection of stories and ideas, sketches and illustrations, I had nothing that would work as a book and had to switch tack a little. Devoting a little more time to my ideas, I eventually pulled a number of things together into the urban fantasy novel, *Blood and Earth*, the first book using the magician characters, Faye Bishop and Joshua Pope. This was published in 2020.

Although I fully intended to follow it with a sequel, my next two books were actually aimed at children:

an illustrated novel called *The Quinton Quads and the Mystery of Malprentice Manor* and a picture book called *Amanda Alexander and the Very Friendly Panda*.

I wasn't leaving games behind, though, and continued to work on a number of projects as well as writing two new books on game writing: *An Introduction to Game Writing* and *201 Things for Better Game Writing*.

While I didn't enter this year thinking that I'll retire from games in 2024, the desire to work on my book ideas grew stronger all the time and (semi-)retirement felt like it was more and more the right thing to do.

I made the announcement with plenty of time to go because I didn't want to drop a bombshell at the last minute on any of my current clients and I hope to finish a few game projects before it's completely final.

I'm also going to publish one last game-related book in which I collect all of the articles I've written over the last two decades. If nothing else, it will serve as handy reference for myself.

My retirement is not about looking to the past, as important as that is, but looking to a future filled with further creativity. I have so many books I want to write, many of which I'll also illustrate, from sequels of the already released titles to new ideas like the children's book I'm currently working on about a young werewolf.

I'll remain around on social media and I'm always happy to engage with people. I hope that those who have enjoyed my work in the games they've played will also follow it in the future by reading my stories.

Thanks to all of you.

PS: I won't entirely turn my back on games as they'll always be fun to play. So I'm hoping to return to Pixel Refresh in the future to share some gaming memories and pop into the Game & Gadget Podcast now and again. Keep your eyes peeled.

Further Information

About the Author

Born and raised in Hull, Steve studied Astronomy and Astrophysics at Newcastle University before taking on jobs as varied as bingo hall management and metal refinery worker. At the age of thirty five he joined the games industry as an artist and has developed this creative career ever since, now working as a freelance writer and artist.

Steve gained a nomination for Excellence in Writing at the Game Developers Choice Awards in 2004 for *Broken Sword: The Sleeping Dragon* and received a second nomination in 2008 from the Writers' Guild of Great Britain for his writing on *So Blonde*.

Steve's book, *Writing for Video Games*, was published by A&C Black and has sold throughout the world, sometimes used as a text in game writing courses. This has recently been followed by the books, *An Introduction to Game Writing* and *201 Things for Better Game Writing* with *Collected Game Writing Articles* making a fourth.

Regularly invited to speak at conferences around the world, Steve enjoys sharing his knowledge and experience.

Steve has also written and drawn a number of online comic strips involving adults, children and a variety of cute animals.

His short film, *Payment*, was released a few years ago to critical acclaim.

He has written a number of fiction books in different styles, including an urban fantasy novel, two children's titles that he also illustrated and a graphic novel. He undertakes illustration work for other writers, too.

He has been working on a climate change app aimed at young children but is now concentrating his creativity on further books, both writing and illustrating.

Other Books by Steve Ince

Non-fiction
Writing for Video Games

An Introduction to Game Writing - A Workbook for Interactive Stories

201 Things for Better Game Writing

Fiction
The Quinton Quads and the Mystery of Malprentice Manor

Blood and Earth

Amanda Alexander and the Very Friendly Panda

Story to Nowhere

Mr. Smoozles: No One Tells Me Anything

Illustration
The Magic Snowflake by Jean Maye and Steve Ince

The Doll's House by Jean Maye

Website and Social Media

Website

www.steve-ince.co.uk

Facebook

Steve.Ince.01

Twitter

@Steve_Ince

Instagram

steveincexl5

LinkedIn

www.linkedin.com/in/stince/

Mastodon

@SInce

TikTok

steveince410

Printed in Great Britain
by Amazon

41008215R00086